ON THE EDGE

Cees Steijger

About the author
Cees Steijger (1955) is a full-time aviation historian and journalist. He is the author of the book *A History of USAFE* about the European operations of the U.S. Army Air Corps/U.S. Army Air Forces and U.S. Air Forces in Europe between 1917 and 1990. He wrote numerous articles about the American forces in Europe during World War II and wrote the book *Crazy Horse* about B-17G 42-30280 of the 482nd Bombardment Group during Operation Argument. The four-part series *On the Edge* is about the Cold War and the role of the U.S. Air Force during various crises. Cees and his wife Kitty have three children and live in Zeewolde, the Netherlands.

Aviation History Research & Publishing

Photo acknowledgment

Most photographs in this publication are from the United States Air Force (USAF) archives, the National Archives and Records Administration (NARA), and other public records. The photographs in this book are individually credited.

Every reasonable effort has been made to trace copyright holders and obtain their permission to use the photo material. The publisher apologizes for errors or omissions in this work and would be grateful if notified of any corrections that should be incorporated in future reprints or editions of this book.

Copyright © 2023 - All rights reserved.

No part of this book may be reproduced or transmitted in any form or by any means, electronic or mechanical, including photocopying, recording, or any information storage and retrieval system, without the publisher's permission in writing.

Book proposals

Aviation History Research & Publishing welcomes book proposals in fields appropriate for Aviation History's editorial program.
Please see our Proposal Submission Guidelines page on our website for more information about how to craft your proposal and what to include: www.aviationhistory.nl/submission
Send your proposal to: editor@aviationhistory.nl

Photo: Walter Sanders/The LIFE Picture Collection/Shutterstock.

Contents

The race is on	-	Page 9
Clash over Trieste	-	Page 20
Global capability	-	Page 28
Soviet conduct	-	Page 40
Operation Vittles	-	Page 49
U.S. Deterrence	-	Page 68
Notes	-	Page 86
Index	-	Page 88

On the Edge

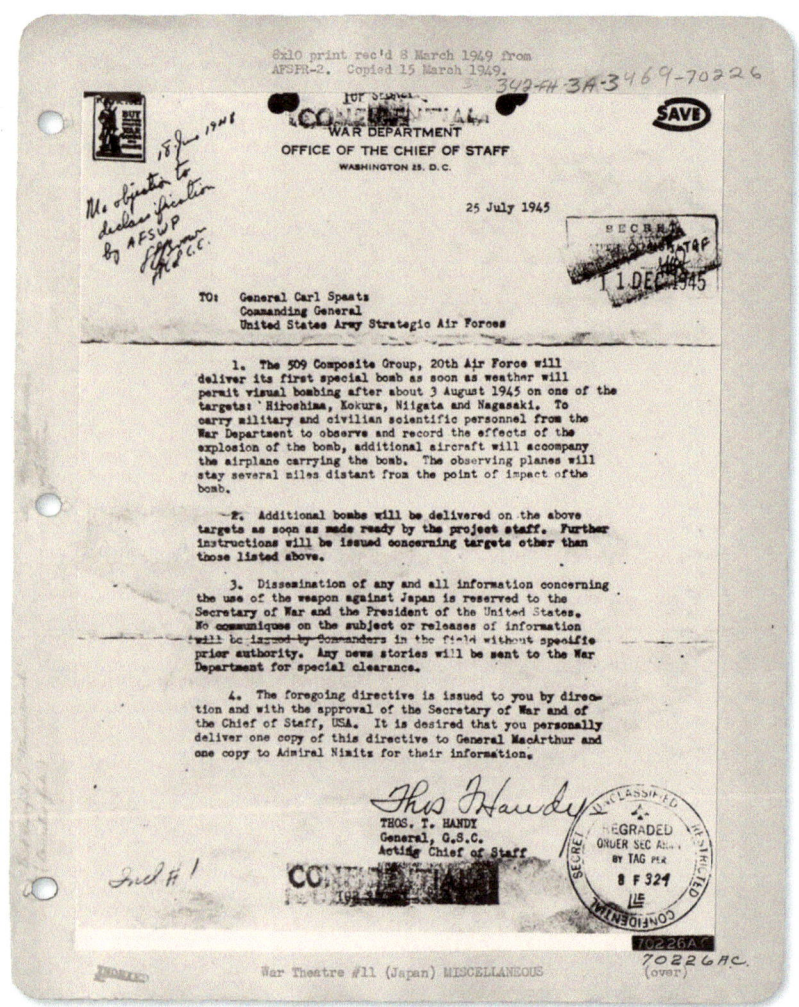

On July 25, 1945, General Carl Spaatz, commander of the U.S. Strategic Air Forces in the Pacific, received orders from General Thomas T. Handy to deliver "Its first special bomb." The 509th Composite Group* on Tinian Island carried out the order on August 6, 1945, by detonating a 20-kiloton uranium bomb over Hiroshima.
Photo: National Archives and Records Administration (NARA).

* The 509th Composite Group was redesignated 509th Bombardment Group (Very Heavy), on June 10, 1946.

On July 25, 1945, General Carl Spaatz, leading the U.S. Strategic Air Forces in the Pacific, received a fateful order: to launch a nuclear attack on Japan. Following the command, the 509th Composite Group stationed on Tinian Island executed the directive on August 6, deploying a 20-kiloton uranium bomb that devastated Hiroshima. Merely three days later, Nagasaki met a similar fate and was also reduced to ruins. During the Allied Forces conference at Potsdam on June 17, 1945, U.S President Harry Truman briefed Joseph Stalin, the secretary general of the Communist Party of the Soviet Union, on the remarkable progress made in American nuclear advancements. Promptly thereafter, Stalin ordered the acceleration of Russia's atomic program. This marked the beginning of a race between the two superpowers, inflaming a Cold War between the capitalist and Communist worlds that was fueled by a toxic mix of distrust, fear and expansionism.

No single event can be considered the beginning of the Cold War. But there are plenty of leads. Even before the end of the war, there were clear signs of rising tension. The friction became visible during the Allied negotiations in Yalta and Potsdam, in which the postwar world was discussed and agreements were made about postwar reparations from Germany. At the Potsdam Conference, one of the highly contentious issues involved the revision of German-Soviet-Polish borders and the subsequent expulsion of millions of Germans from the disputed regions. The issue of Poland had already been a prominent topic of discussion during previous allied conferences. As part of the settlement, Poland was to receive compensation in the west, gaining substantial territories from Germany extending up to the Oder-Neisse Line, which followed the course of the Oder and Neisse Rivers. Meanwhile, Germany and Berlin itself would be divided into four zones under Allied occupation.

The "Big Three" Allied leaders, Attlee, Stalin, and Truman, left the Potsdam conference in August 1945 satisfactorily and posed in a cheerful mood for the press photographers. The former Allies felt relieved and looked forward to peace and security after six years of war. However, the calm and peace among the Western Allies proved short-lived. While the armies of the Western world were quickly disbanded, the Soviet Union kept its army at war strength and maintained its strategic positions in Eastern Europe and the Far East. By threatening military action, which it could successfully carry out because of its military power, the Soviet Union imposed its will on its neighboring countries. It put such pressure on Western nations that they yielded on crucial political issues. U.S. and Soviet interests were coming into opposition. It was an ideological battle between Russian communism and capitalism in the democratic Western nations.

This book is part one of the series on U.S. Air Force reactions during the Cold War; author Cees Steijger examines the circumstances under which some events brought the world to the brink of a third world war. During the Cold War between East and West, humanity lived on the edge of collapse, only narrowly escaping the apocalypse a few times.

Cees Steijger
Zeewolde, Netherlands
September 2023

Chapter One

The race is on

Shortly after Germany capitulated in May 1945, the United States began demobilizing its Air Force in Europe. In late May, the War Department ordered the U.S. Strategic Air Forces in Europe (USSAFE) to send all remaining flyable, heavy-bombardment aircraft and their crews back to the United States, except for aircraft earmarked for the occupation. Within four weeks of redeployment, over 62,000 men left the European theater. By mid-August, the command had redeployed 1,200 airplanes and 144,000 personnel—almost one-third of its total force.

The aim was to maintain a tiny European organization, exclusively for communication and transport purposes. The European theater commander, General Joseph T. McNarney, said: "All I require is an Air Force of about 7,500 personnel to provide transport and communications."[1] This was a far cry from the 17,000 aircraft and an organization of around half a million men that USSAFE commanded at the war's end in Europe. Many airmen and most flying equipment in the United Kingdom and the liberated countries were redeployed to the U.S. or transferred to the Pacific theater. In November 1945, McNarney took over the position of Commanding General from Dwight D. Eisenhower, who was appointed the Chief of Staff of the Army in Washington D.C. Eisenhower, at whom McNarney's proclamation was aimed, thought the same way. Although the State Department voiced some concern about such a drastic reduction of air power in Europe, it withdrew its objections and the phased reduction continued.

The Polish question

The optimism of the U.S. military command that steered the rapid demobilization was in sharp contrast to political developments in Europe at the time. American-Russian differences which, paradoxically, appeared negligible during the war when they were fighting a common enemy, came to the fore again in 1945. The basis for the differences originated at Yalta in February 1945 during a summit conference between the Big Three (America, Russia, and Britain). Yalta was the last in a series of summit conferences and followed Casablanca, Quebec, Moscow, and Teheran. It was also the most important meeting between the Big Three in wartime. During the Yalta conference, Roosevelt, Churchill, and Stalin discussed postwar borders, set German reparation payments and decided to occupy the whole of Germany. Berlin, the former capital of the Third Reich and Ger-

July 16, 1945, at 5:29:45 a.m., a light "brighter than a thousand suns" filled the valley of the Alamogordo desert in southern New Mexico. The first atomic explosion code-named Trinity, was a success for the American WWII Manhattan Project for the development of nuclear arms. Photo: Collection Harry S. Truman Library & Museum.

Chapter One - **The Race is on**

Photo of the last meeting of the Potsdam Conference in Potsdam, Germany, on August 1, 1945. President Harry S. Truman is seated around the conference table on the right side of the table. Secretary of State James Byrnes is sitting to the President's right hand. Admiral William Leahy is seated to the right hand of Mr. Byrnes. Generalissimo Joseph Stalin of the Soviet Union is wearing a white uniform and is seated at the top of the table. Vyacheslav Molotov, Soviet foreign minister, is sitting in the photo to the left of Stalin. British Prime Minister Clement Attlee (who became prime minister during the conference, replacing Winston Churchill) is at the bottom left side of the table in the photo. Photo: U.S. National Archives and Records Administration (NARA).

many itself, were divided into occupation zones.

Germany was roughly divided geographically into a Western Zone and an Eastern Zone. The eastern zone was Russia's while the Western Zone was divided between America and Britain. Berlin, which lay in the Russian zone, was also divided in this way. Later, France, which had vainly asked to participate in the Yalta summit, was granted occupation zones in Germany and Berlin which were formed out of the American and British occupation zones.

One of the core problems during the Yalta conference was Poland. The complex "Polish question" was to become a large stumbling block in the relationships between the Allies. As far as the Russians were concerned, the matter was simple: Poland had in the past attacked Russia more than once and must be brought into the Russian sphere of influence and Poland's Western borders must be redrawn according to the Soviet proposal along the Rivers Oder and Western Neisse, including Swinemünde and Stettin. And, said the Soviet delegation, the new Polish government must be unequivocally pro-Russian. The Western Allies rightly continued to press for democratic government and free elections. Russia also laid claim to a large area of Polish territory in the eastern part of the country. A compromise seemed impossible. Russia's power position was clear: The Red Armies had liberated Poland and, therefore, Poland's future was a matter for the Russians to decide.

Truman's hard line

On April 12, 1945, one month after the Yalta summit, President Roosevelt died. His successor, the hardnosed, anti-Communist Harry S. Truman, showed his displeasure about the Polish question almost immediately upon taking office. The American line hardened and the more relaxed American-Russian relationship desired by Roosevelt was put under pressure. The meeting between Truman and Vyacheslav Molotov, the Russian Minister for Foreign Affairs, which took place in San Francisco on April 23, 1945, is generally accepted as having had a great influence on the development of events. Truman took Molotov to task and told him bluntly that Russia must comply with the principal agreement of Yalta regarding Poland. In emphatic tones, Truman stated that the U.S. wanted friendship with Russia but that friendship could only be based on mutual observance of agreements and not on the basis of "one-way traffic."

An apparently astounded Molotov said that he had never been talked to like that in his life. "Carry out your agreements, and you won't get talked to like that," was Truman's answer. Truman's interpreter, Charles E. Bohlen, was later to write in his book *Witness to History* that he had never seen such a fierce slanging match from a highly placed official. The U.S. atomic program had made good progress, and that made Truman confident. The prospect for the U.S. was a nuclear monopoly as long as the Soviet Union did not have an atomic bomb. This situation explains Truman's self-assurance and uncompromising stance.

On August 7, 1945, The War Department deleted the word "strategic" from the USSAFE command title, and it became the United States Air Forces in Europe (USAFE).[2]

The final punch

Three weeks earlier, the United States Strategic Air Forces in the Pacific organization was activated and organized for the final punch. While in Europe, the U.S. forces were rapidly phased out, in the Pacific, the fighting was still intense, and pressure on Japan was growing; the preparations for a nuclear attack were in top gear. In July, the U.S. managed to deliver the uranium and plutonium cores and material for assembling two atomic bombs to Tinian Island. Tinian is one of the Mariana Islands in the Pacific Ocean, approximately 1,500 miles (2,400 kilometers) south of Tokyo. The heavy cruiser USS Indianapolis of the U.S. Navy shipped most of the nuclear material of the Little Boy uranium bomb. At the same time, Douglas C-54 transport planes of the 509th Composite Group flew in the parts and components of the Fat Man plutonium bomb. The small island of Tinian was the Twentieth Air Force's busiest airfield. It was the world's largest airfield with four 8,000 feet (2,438 meters) runways and hardstands for 238 B-29 Superfortress four-engine heavy bombers. It was home to the 509th Composite Group equipped with 15 specially modified B-29s, each capable of delivering an atomic bomb. These modified bombers became America's first nuclear launch aircraft. They arrived between July 4 and 6 on the North Field airfield on Tinian. After a brief training period and practicing maneuvers with dummy atomic bomb deliveries, the 509th was ready for the world's first nuclear attack.

On August 6, a modified Boeing B-29 Superfortress nicknamed Enola Gay took off from Tinian. The cargo consisted of the heavy uranium bomb nicknamed Little Boy. The bomb was 120 inches (300 centimeters) in length, 28 inches (71 centimeters) in diameter, and weighed approximately 9,700 pounds (4,400 kilograms). It contained 141 pounds (64 kilograms) of highly enriched uranium U235. Piloted by Colonel Paul W. Tibbets, the commander of the 509th Bombardment Group, the B-29 took off at 2:45 a.m. and set course northwest, heading for the Japanese city of Hiroshima. Located on the deltas of southwestern Honshu Island facing the Inland Sea, it was 1,361 nautical miles (2,521 kilometers) away from Tinian. The target area was reached five hours later when Tibbets started to climb to 31,000 feet for its bomb run.

At approximately 8:15 a.m. Hiroshima time, Little Boy was released. Forty-four seconds later, 15 kilotons of TNT detonated at 1,900 feet (600 meters) above the city. In a matter of seconds, Little Boy wiped away most of Hiroshima, killing an estimated 66,000 people of its population of 255,000 and injuring another 69,000. By the end of 1945, the Hiroshima death toll rose to 140,000 as radiation sickness deaths mounted. Five years later the total reached 200,000.[3]

Fat Man

Three days after the Armageddon of Hiroshima, on August 9, 1945, a Boeing B-29 nicknamed Bock's Car, piloted by the 393rd Heavy Bombardment Squadron's commander, Major Charles W. Sweeney, lifted off at 3:47 a.m. from Tinian. Sweeney was heading for the primary target, Kokura Arsenal, located on

Chapter One - **The Race is on**

the northern coast of Kyushu Island. On board was the second U.S. atomic bomb called Fat Man which was similar in length as Little Boy, but had more than twice its diameter. Sweeney found unacceptable weather conditions over the target area and was welcomed with flak when he arrived above Kokura.

After three unsuccessful bomb runs over the city, Sweeney decided to switch to the secondary target Nagasaki. This city on the island of Kyushu was home to the Mitsubishi plant that had manufactured the torpedoes used at Pearl Harbor. At Nagasaki, there was a thick overcast which only allowed for the bomb run to be made by radar. At the last minute, a brief break in the cloud cover made a visual targeting at 29,000 feet possible and Bock's Car dropped her single payload, a fission bomb weighing 10,300 pounds (4,700 kilograms) at 11:01 a.m. Fat Man's 14.1 pounds (6.4 kilograms) Plutonium-239 exploded 1,650 feet (502 meters) above the slopes of the city with a force of 21,000 tons of TNT. Fat Man instantly killed 40,000 people and injured 60,000 more. By January 1946, 70,000 people had died in Nagasaki. Five years later the total eventually reached 140,000.[4]

After the nuclear strike on Hiroshima, the Japanese supreme command cloaked itself in silence. They struggled to come to a decision, with military extremists in their midst continuing to advocate a policy of resistance to the end. With Hiroshima and Nagasaki significantly wiped away, the Japanese leadership feared the frightening prospect that the B-29s from Tinian would attack more Japanese cities with devastating atomic bombs. President Harry Truman had the Japanese cities Kokura Arsenal, Niigata, and Kyoto[5] on his target list but held up a third atomic attack while the United States considered a Japanese response. Word finally reached Washington from Switzerland and Sweden early on August 10 that the Japanese, according to Hirohito's wishes, would accept the surrender terms, provided the emperor retained his position.[6] The war was over; the Cold War was about to begin.

The Manhattan Project

The two atomic bombs that ended the second World War were significant milestones in an evolutionary physics science process that eventually led to the Manhattan Project to develop nuclear energy. Between September 17, 1942 and December 31, 1946, more than 130,000 scientists, specialists, developers, technicians, etc. worked under the leadership of Brigadier General Leslie R. Groves in covert and remote locations throughout the country. The project costs were estimated at U.S. $2 billion (equivalent to about U.S. $23 billion in 2022). Over ninety percent of the cost was for building factories for the production of fissile material, with less than ten percent for the development and production of the weapons. Research and production took place at more than thirty sites across the United States, the United Kingdom, and Canada. And urgency was required because of similar developments in Nazi Germany. Allied intelligence reports indicated that Germany was rapidly making progress. It was common knowledge that fission had been discovered in Nazi Germany almost three years earlier and that since spring 1940, a large part of the Kaiser Wilhelm Institute in Berlin had been set aside for uranium research. The German nuclear development took place under the leadership of the physicist Werner Heisenberg who in 1932 received a Nobel prize for his contribution to quantum mechanics.

At the Alamogordo Bombing Range, known as the Jornada del Muerto—the "Journey of Death", by the Spanish conquistadores—in New Mexico, at half past five on the morning of July 16, 1945, a bright flash of light was followed by an explosion of unprecedented power. After nearly three years of feverish work, Robert Oppenheimer, Head of the Atomic Laboratory in Los Alamos, and his team had succeeded in detonating the world's first atomic bomb. The result of this test explosion was beyond even the most optimistic expectations. Shortly after the blinding atomic flash, an enormous cloud of smoke and flames mushroomed into the

Opposite page: Demobilization in June 1945. North American P-51 Mustangs of the 78th Fighter Group at RAF Duxford, England. Most of these fighters went back to the United States. Also, many of these surplus aircraft were used to re-arm the Western air forces. Photo: U.S. Air Force.

Chapter One - **The Race is on**

Due to political objections, there were no bases in France and England for the USAAF's atomic B-29s, nor were there any nuclear facilities for the USAAF in the American occupied countries. Conventional bombers were not strangers in the European skies. In March 1944, a B-29 visited the U.S. Eighth Air Force. The YB-29, serial number 41-36393, nicknamed Hobo Queen, was in England for evaluation flights and a show of force along U.S. airfields. It was mainly a piece of disinformation intended for the Germans to make them believe that the Americans would deploy heavy B-29s to Europe. However, that didn't happen. The first time a B-29 appeared over the European continent was on September 5, 1945, when a brand new Superfortress with serial number 44-61679 landed at Orly, Paris, France. After Paris, the B-29 also appeared at Schiphol Airport near Amsterdam in the Netherlands and at Kastrup near Copenhagen, Denmark. On October 8, the B-29 completed its European propaganda tour with a visit to RAF Bovingdon, northwest of London, near Eighth Air Force HQ at Bushy Park, as seen in the picture above. Photo: U.S. Army Air Force.

air. The wave of air pressure was so great that everything within a radius of 5,250 feet (1,600 meters) was blown away, and even outside this circle, the destruction was considerable.

He asked nothing!

America was, literally, in a flash, not only financially and economically but also militarily, the most powerful nation in the world.

The day after he took office, Truman was briefed by his advisor James F. Byrnes on American nuclear developments. According to Byrnes, the United States would be able to hold onto its atomic monopoly for six to seven years. During that time, Russia would be forced to accept America's plans for world peace. In his memoirs, Truman wrote that, according to Byrnes, possessing the atom bomb gave the U.S. power to dictate conditions after the war. So began Truman's Atomic Diplomacy, a diplomacy he put into practice right away during the Potsdam conference, which started on July 17, just a few hours after he was informed about Oppenheimer's success.

Truman waited a week before casually remarking to Stalin that America had a new weapon with unprecedented destructive power. Truman later wrote that Stalin showed no interest and merely remarked that he hoped America could use it usefully against Japan. "He asked nothing," said an astonished Truman to Churchill a short while later.[7] But Stalin didn't have to ask; he knew full well what Truman was "subtly" trying to say. After the conference, Stalin told Molotov that Igor W. Kurchatov, head of the Russian atomic program, to hurry up with his work.[8]

Never trust a fox

Many years later, it became clear why Stalin reacted so understatedly to Truman's seemingly casual remark. Stalin had known about the U.S. nuclear claim since 1943—perhaps earlier. Through the German physicist Dr. Klaus Fuchs, who fled to England, the Russians received detailed information about the Manhattan program.[9] Fuchs was secretly a member of the German Communist Party and was sought by the Gestapo after the Reichstag fire in 1933 and fled to England via France with the help of friends in the French Communist Party. There he received his doctorate from the University of Bristol (Doctorate of Philosophy in mathematical physics) and the University of Edinburgh (Doctorate of Philosophy in mathematical physics). Fuchs was a brilliant nuclear scientist, and his qualities brought him a position in the team of scientists working at the University of Birmingham on the gaseous diffusion process of separating uranium isotopes, which was still in the experimental stage both in Britain and the United States. Fuchs was not told the full nature of the work—he was simply informed that it was urgent, it was secret, and it was connected with the war.

Very soon after he started to work in Birmingham in 1941, he began to pass over information to the Russians.[10] Certainly, he would have been able to tell them that the uranium bomb was a definite possibility. He could have —and in fact, did— give them the results of his own calculations on the theory of the gaseous diffusion process for separating the isotopes of uranium, and the fact that U235 produced in that way might be used in an atomic bomb. He could also have furnished his own calculations of the amount of U235 needed and of the efficiency of the explosion. For sure, Fuchs regularly handed over detailed information when in December 1943, as a member of the British research team, he became part of the Manhattan team of scientists in New York and worked on the gaseous diffusion process and planned future joint British/American operations.[11] Regularly, he would secretly meet with Russian agents and hand over information about the progress and results at the Los Alamos laboratory, where he had worked since the summer of 1944.

Fuchs witnessed the nuclear test on July 16, 1944 and was amazed by the magnitude of the explosion; its enormous flash filled the sky. It was far brighter than anything they had imagined and calculated. The Alamogordo explosion was the beginning of the ending of Anglo-American association over the atomic bomb. The British scientists began winding up their affairs in the United States. Fuchs was also packing his bags. But not before he, on September 19, went out to Santa Fe for his last meeting with his Russian spy. Fuchs had written down all he knew. He gave the size of the bomb—a vital point—what it contained, how it was constructed, and how it was detonated. He gave his own calculations of the actual dimensions of the parts. And he handed all this over in one package.[12]

Russia received almost a blueprint of the American atomic bomb and could speed-up their own efforts to build nuclear deterrent. During the Potsdam conference, Stalin knew it all the way; it was just a matter of time before Russia too would have an atomic bomb. It would take four years for Kurchatov and his team to successfully test a nuclear bomb at the Semipalatinsk Test Site in Kazakhstan. On August 29, 1949, Russia successfully tested its own weapon and became a superpower. It is clear that Fuchs' treason contributed and most certainly shortened the time needed for Russia to develop the atomic bomb. In 1991, the Russian magazine *Molodaya Gvardiya* published an article in which ultra-patriotics criticized the scientific community in Russia. They claimed that there was no Russian atomic bomb. There

The first press reports of a B-29 coming to England was in October 1945. Left a brief article in the issue of Aeroplane Spotter of October 18, 1945.

"Meanwhile, what is to happen about Russia? I feel deep anxiety because of their misinterpretation of the Yalta decisions, their attitude towards Poland, their overwhelming influence in the Balkans, excepting Greece, the difficulties they make about Vienna, the combination of Russian power and the territories under their control or occupied, coupled with the Communist technique in so many other countries, and above all their power to maintain very large armies in the field. What will be the position in a year or two when the British and American Armies have melted and the French have not yet been formed on any major scale... and when Russia may choose to keep two or three hundred divisions on active service? An iron curtain is drawn down upon their front. We do not know what is going on behind. A broad band of many hundreds of miles will isolate us from Poland. Meanwhile, the attention of our peoples will be occupied in inflicting severities upon Germany, which is ruined and prostrate, and it will be open to the Russians in a very short time to advance, if they chose, to the waters of the North Sea and the Atlantic..."

A quote from the British Prime Minister Winston Churchill in a telegram to U.S. President Harry Truman, 15 May 1945.

Chapter One - **The Race is on**

Three Boeing B-29A bombers (serial numbers 45-21747, 45-21750, 45-21751) touched down at RAF Marham in March 1946 to participate in Project Ruby. This was a joint Anglo-American project investigating the use of penetration bombs against heavily-protected concrete targets. Initially, the trials took place on a submarine pen on the island of Helgoland. The B-29s primarily targeted the so called Valentin bunker at Bremer Vulkan on the Weser River with the 22,000-pound Amazon T-2S Semi-Armor-Piercing bomb (the American version of the British Grand Slam bomb). During 1943/44, the vast U-boat bunker Valentin was constructed near the village of Farge. It was supposed to be a heavily protected yard for building submarines, using forced laborers from the large concentration camp Neuengamme near Hamburg. Completed in 1944, the bunker did not realize its intended fast U-boat Type-11 production. In 1946, it provided an excellent test target for heavy bombs. The bunker was hit eight times with the heaviest conventional bombs, but not with much success. Later that year, three modified B-29s participated in Project Harken, dropping 25,000-pound (11,340 kg) conventional test bombs from 17,000 feet on the Valentin bunker. The B-29s were from the 97th Bombardment Group and stationed at Giebelstadt Air Base, Germany, from July 14 to November 4, 1947. The former submarine bunker is currently the second-largest above-ground bunker in Europe; the largest is the German U-boat pens in Saint-Nazaire, France. The photo shows B-29A 42-63577 releasing a 12,000 lb Tallboy earthquake bomb. From March to June 1945, the USAF tested the operational suitability of the B-29 for carrying and releasing 12,000-pound Tallboy bombs at the U.S. Army Proving Ground, Eglin Army Air Field, Florida. Photo: U.S. Army Air Force.

is only an American one masterfully discovered by Soviet spies.[13]

The Russians get their way

To reinforce his words, Truman stopped American Lend-Lease to Russia on May 8, 1945. Ships en route to Russia with food, clothing, weapons, and ammunition were recalled. This economic measure, which was meant to put pressure on Stalin, had the opposite effect: Stalin let Truman know that this attitude made a mutual solution to the Polish question impossible.

This promised little for the Big Three summit meeting due to be held in Potsdam from July 17 to August 2. At Potsdam, where Truman told Stalin of the American nuclear test explosion the day before the summit started, it was decided that the Allied armies would occupy the whole of Germany and, for the time being, the Supreme Commanders of the Allied forces would administer the country. As far as Poland was concerned, the Russians got their own way. East Germany up to the Oder and the Neisse became part of Poland, as did the southern part of East Prussia. These areas came under Polish administration and, therefore, were not seen as part of the Russian occupation zone.

The Western Allies were emphatic that these Polish borders were only accepted conditionally; the definite borders were to be settled during a peace conference to be held at a later date, but because the Western Allies did agree that the entire German population should be removed from the areas allocated to Poland, it was impossible to talk of a "temporary" border agreement. Stalin must have come to the same conclusion. Western influence was gone from East Germany and Poland. At Potsdam, Europe was dealt out like a pack of cards—the name of the game for decades afterwards was world tension.

Lighter and faster: Silverplate B-29

By the end of World War II, some 4,000 B-29s would be operational. But only a small number of them were able to perform as atomic bombers. To accommodate the weight of a five-ton atomic bomb, engineers, under the supervision of Colonel Tibbets, developed a fleet of specially designed B-29 bombers. These so called Silverplate B-29s were made lighter and faster by removing all gun turrets except for the rear one and by eliminating much of their protective armored plating. Faster engines with reversible pitch propellers (enabling the plane to taxi in reverse) were added.[14] To drop the much larger atomic weapon, the bomb bay doors were enlarged and pneumatically driven, allowing faster opening and closing at the point of delivery.

The technology for those modifications they found in Great Britain, where the Royal Air Force (RAF) had experience in delivering heavyweight bombs such as the Grand Slam. The bomb hoist, shackle, and rack system big enough to hold the American atomic bomb were bought in Britain.[15] Eventually, the Americans switched to U.S. manufactured equipment, but the original B-29s that were atomic capable had British racks and shackles.

Lack of nuclear facilities

By 1946, the U.S. Army Air Force had twenty-seven Silverplates, and in 1948, the total number of modified B-29s was thirty-two, with only twelve fully trained crews. It should be considered that the U.S. had eleven stockpiled nuclear warheads by the year-end of 1946.[16] None of them were in Europe. Besides, no Silverplate B-29 of the 509th Bombardment Group, the only unit with operational nuclear bombers, could be armed at any air base in Europe, not in Germany or Great Britain. Some bases had runways strong, long, and wide enough to handle the heavy-weight Silverplates, such as RAF Marham, RAF Scampton, RAF Lakenheath,

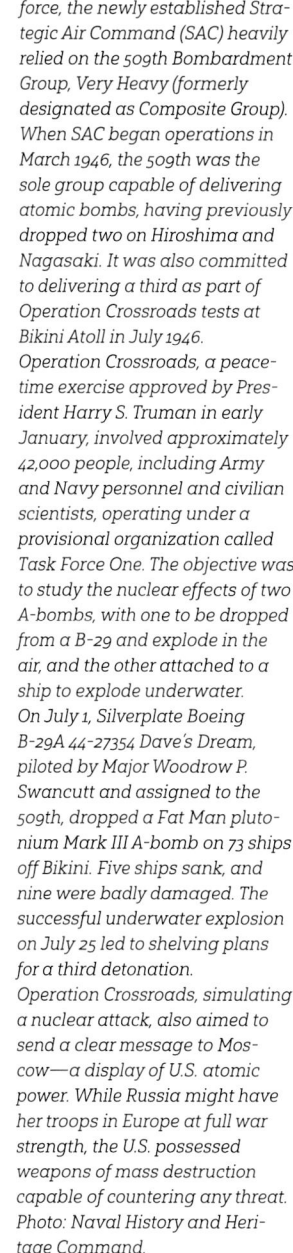

In developing a nuclear bombing force, the newly established Strategic Air Command (SAC) heavily relied on the 509th Bombardment Group, Very Heavy (formerly designated as Composite Group). When SAC began operations in March 1946, the 509th was the sole group capable of delivering atomic bombs, having previously dropped two on Hiroshima and Nagasaki. It was also committed to delivering a third as part of Operation Crossroads tests at Bikini Atoll in July 1946. Operation Crossroads, a peacetime exercise approved by President Harry S. Truman in early January, involved approximately 42,000 people, including Army and Navy personnel and civilian scientists, operating under a provisional organization called Task Force One. The objective was to study the nuclear effects of two A-bombs, with one to be dropped from a B-29 and explode in the air, and the other attached to a ship to explode underwater. On July 1, Silverplate Boeing B-29A 44-27354 Dave's Dream, piloted by Major Woodrow P. Swancutt and assigned to the 509th, dropped a Fat Man plutonium Mark III A-bomb on 73 ships off Bikini. Five ships sank, and nine were badly damaged. The successful underwater explosion on July 25 led to shelving plans for a third detonation. Operation Crossroads, simulating a nuclear attack, also aimed to send a clear message to Moscow—a display of U.S. atomic power. While Russia might have her troops in Europe at full war strength, the U.S. possessed weapons of mass destruction capable of countering any threat. Photo: Naval History and Heritage Command.

Chapter One - **The Race is on**

The U.S. Joint Intelligence Committee initially proposed attacks against seventeen Russian cities. Subsequently, the U.S. Joint War Plans Committee reduced the original list of twenty, excluding three cities—Leningrad, Sverdlovsk, and Nizhni Tagil—either due to being beyond the B-29 range or deemed of insufficient strategic value. The directive within the target cities was to focus on destroying industrial facilities, particularly aircraft and ordnance factories, governmental administration complexes, and scientific research centers. The plan assumed a delivery accuracy of forty-eight percent for all airborne atomic bombs. The bombing strategy called for ninety-eight atomic bombs with an additional one hundred held in reserve, totaling 196 weapons. Source: American War Plans 1945-1950.

RAF Mildenhall, and RAF Bassingbourne and in Germany, the air bases Rhein-Main (Frankfurt), Giebelstadt (Würzburg) and Fürstenfeldbruck (Munich). But all these bases lacked the facilities to accommodate the storage, assembly, and arming of the nuclear Mark III Fat Man plutonium bomb. Also, rather important, none of these bases had the storage pit to enable assembly teams to hoist the Mark III in place.[17]

Building nuclear bases

In Italy in late 1945, near the Italian city of Foggia, work was proceeding apace on an airfield to make it suitable for using B-29 nuclear bombers. It was at the strategically located Amendola air base, part of the vast military complex near Foggia that included numerous airfields during World War II, somewhat similar to East Anglia in England, which was dotted with air bases, installations, and depots too. During the war, the Fifteenth Air Force used the base as the station for two B-17 Flying Fortress heavy-bomber groups. The U.S. engineers used some 4,000 German prisoners of war to build several ammunition depots and to construct the B-29 pits for loading the atomic bombs. At the same time, the runway was extended and reinforced to accommodate the heavy B-29 Superfortresses.

By September 1946, the base was ready for deployment, perhaps as Europe's first operational U.S. nuclear base. In any event, it became one of the largest combat air bases in Italy. In a news report, United Press cited Air Force officers saying the field was ready for immediate use as Italy's main U.S. occupational air base. Similar work also took place on the other side of the world. The three major occupied air bases in Japan, Yokota and Wissawa, and Kadena on Okinawa, were equally being upgraded to host the heavy B-29 bombers.

Soviets could strike at any time

The establishment of American nuclear bases in Europe and Asia was not a luxury. In America's view, after the fall of Germany, the Soviets' intentions were still toward expansion. And although the big three were still acting together as Allies against Nazi Germany during the war, the Soviets feared capitalist encirclement and would try to dominate Eastern Europe and other states on their border. And they wanted access to warm water ports, hence their pressure on Greece, Turkey, and Iran. The Soviets were even putting pressure on Norway for concessions on Spitsbergen. In October 1945, the U.S. Joint Strategic Survey Committee, the former U.S. Joint War Plans Committee, advised the U.S. Joint Chiefs of Staff on postwar stability. Like the Americans, the Russians were quickly demobilizing the Soviet Union. But Moscow intended to maintain substantial peacetime forces. The committee's report estimated that the Soviet Union, with over four million troops under arms, had the military capability to overrun Western Europe and the Middle East between 1945 and 1948. In early 1946, the Soviets had forty-two armed divisions in (Eastern) Germany in high readiness, supported by four thousand combat aircraft. They could strike at any time and without warning, reaching the river Rhine in one day and overrunning the U.S. zone of occupation in five days. Korea would wait for the same fate, while the Soviets would crush Turkey in less than half a year.[18]

JCS stesses early use of atomic weapons

Although the U.S. had a nuclear capability, which the Soviets at that time did not, the JSSC noted that the U.S. in 1945 lacked sufficient atomic bombs to effectively attack and destroy Soviet transportation networks and power grids. Besides, strategic nuclear weapons were less valuable on battlefields because of the limited numbers available.[19] Nevertheless, the U.S. Joint Chiefs of Staff stressed the early use of atomic weapons in any war with the Soviet Union. The Air Corps would launch a nuclear strike aimed at the Soviet war industry in twenty major cities throughout the USSR. For the execution of that strike, an estimated 196 A-bombs would be necessary. The committee had made a priority list that included Moscow, Gorki, Kuibyshev (Samara), Sverdlovsk, Novosibirsk, Omsk, Saratov, Kazan, Leningrad (St. Petersburg), Baku, Tashkent, Chelyabinsk, Nizhni Tagil, Magnitogorsk, Molotov (Perm), Tbilisi, Stalinsk (Novokoeznetsk), Grozny, Irkutsk, and Yaroslavl.[20] B-29s had to operate from bases in England, Italy, India, and China to reach these targets. There were only two major problems with this approach: the combat radius of the B-29 was 2,000 miles (3,218 kilometers), which meant that not all targets were within reach. The majority of the USSR was, in fact, out of reach for the American bombers. And the other problem was the lack of detailed target data. Notably, the targets east of Moscow were potential disasters; bomber crews would locate targets navigating on Tsarist maps![21]

Industrial priority targets* in the USSR
The U.S. concept for war plan *Pincher*, March 2, 1946.

*Names of cities in 1946

On March 2, 1946, the Joint War Plans Committee (JWPC) published a paper entitled "Concept of Operations for Pincher." With Pincher, U.S. strategists laid the groundwork for contingency plans to address the possibility of a global conflict. Pincher underwent continuous updates and served as a strategic blueprint in the event of the U.S. entering World War III. Pincher asserted that any conflict or war with the USSR, regardless of its origin, would escalate into a total global conflict. The planners assumed that Soviet aggression would be concentrated in the Middle East, specifically targeting the Suez Canal, with the aim of controlling the Eastern Mediterranean and Persian Gulf oil resources. The European continent was deemed indefensible. British, French, and American occupation forces would likely be unable to withstand a Soviet offensive, doing little more than delaying the Red Army at the Rhine. American forces would establish and defend bases in the British Isles, Egypt, Pakistan, India, Italy, and Western China. From these bases, allied forces would launch strikes against the war industry in the USSR and destroy the Soviet war and merchant fleet. Pincher included a list of thirty industrial centers in the Soviet Union. These urban targets comprised the twenty cities designated by the Joint Intelligence Committee in November 1945, with the JWPC adding ten more.
Source: American War Plans 1945-1950.

Chapter Two
Clash over Trieste

The lack of target information was a significant issue for the Americans. There was simply no recent photo material available of the Russian targets for nuclear precision bombing. Now, a devastating twenty-ton TNT atomic bomb does not have to fall precisely on its target, but at least it had to be close to it. Shortly after World War II, USAFE began a series of European reconnaissance flights that led to numerous skirmishes and high tension. These clandestine, covert reconnaissance missions were nicknamed Ferret flights and began in 1946.

During World War II, the American photographic and observation groups in England regularly carried out photo flights over Germany. These reconnaissance flights not only provided American Fighter Command with a clear picture of the bomb damage sustained by German industry but also enabled strategic German targets to be put on the map.

American aerial espionage did not stop once the war in Europe was over. On the contrary, in the second half of 1945 the number of reconnaissance flights increased. Within this framework, the Air Force's task changed from strategic bombing—unnecessary since Germany's surrender—to air intelligence and aerial

Yugoslav fighters shot down a C-47 Skytrain, similar to the one depicted here. During the war, C-47s were used in large numbers and played a significant role in the 1944 invasion. In wartime, 43-15075 was part of the 313th Troop Carrier Group of the Ninth Air Force. It participated in Operation Overlord on June 6, 1944, transporting paratroopers from the 82nd Airborne Division. Postwar, C-47s were extensively utilized by USAFE for transport, liaison, and reconnaissance operations. The C-47's official name was Skytrain, but its crew affectionately referred to the aircraft as the Gooney Bird.
Photo: Author's collection.

mapping. Between the autumn of 1945 and the summer of 1947, the U.S. Air Force carried out a series of projects, during which areas in west and central Europe, North Africa, and the Atlantic islands were mapped for future military use. Also in the Pacific, extensive photomapping was carried out; the 311th Reconnaissance Wing had six photomapping squadrons of which three were performing photomapping over Korea, Japan, and China. Among the aircraft used most by the U.S. Air Force for photomapping were RB-24 Liberators, RB-17 Flying Fortresses, and RB-29s (originally designated F-7, F-9, and F-13 respectively). These were converted World War II bombers fitted with a large number of cameras. One extensive mapping project was code-named Casey Jones and took place in Europe. Casey Jones reconnaissance flights were only supposed to be flown over the Western Allies' occupation zones but the American Information Service has never released any information about these flights and there is a strong suspicion that the reconnaissance aircraft also operated over the Russian occupation zone. Specially modified and camera-carrying Boeing RB-17s (F-9) conducted periodic photo missions along the Soviet borders from the Baltic to the Black Sea. Vital and fruitful were photo and ELINT (Electronic Intelligence) in the Berlin air corridors, the air routes from Western Germany to the divided city of Berlin. Observations of Soviet activity in the Russian-occupied part of Germany were perfectly legal. This aerial reconnaissance was a significant source of intelligence. For these spy missions, Douglas RB-26 (F-3) Invader bombers and Douglas C-47 Skytrain transports were fitted with cameras. In contrast, outdated Boeing B-17 bombers were converted for both photo and ELINT work along the Soviet-controlled borders in Europe.[22]

Russia opens fire

Russian fighters regularly opened fire on American aircraft caught over the Russian occupation zones, and time and again, the U.S. Air Transport Command (ATC) C-47 Skytrains were involved. For example, on April 22, 1946, an American C-47A was attacked by Red Army Bell P-39 Airacobra fighters near Tulln/Langenlebarn air base (currently Fliegerhorst Brumowski) flying northwest of the air base but over the Soviet-occupied zone. Tulln became an important transport hub between Germany, Italy, and the Mediterranean for the allied occupation forces. The U.S. European Air Transport Service (EATS) provided transport capacity. The EATS had its headquarters and operational and maintenance facilities at Capodichino near Napels for its Mediterranean operations. The 305th Troop Carrier Squadron provided transport services in the Mediterranean. From its base at Capodichino, the 305th connected Vienna, Udine, Pisa, and Rome with daily flight operations with C-47 Skytrain transport aircraft. The 305th played a vital role in the final phase of the war when, as part of the 442nd Troop Carrier Group, its primary mission was to fly gasoline and other critical supplies to the ground forces, which were driving deep into the heart of Germany. Forward landing fields, often within the range of the enemy lines, were used as delivery points for the millions of pounds of supplies that the group ferried during the final three months of war in 1945.[23] In August 1946, merely twelve months after the war ended, they were likely unaware of the potential danger involved in the flights between Udine in northern Italy and Vienna, where their flight plans carried them close to Yugoslav airspace.

On August 19, 1946, an unarmed C-47 lost its way during bad weather and inadvertently flew over Yugoslav territory. Without sufficient forewarning, the plane was shot down by Vladimir Vodopivec, a pilot in the Yugoslav Air Force, flying a Yak-3. All five on board were killed. The C-47 Skytrain was from the 305th Troop Carrier Squadron (Riem/Munich Air Base) and made a flight from Tulln to Udine in Italy.
Photo: Author's collection.

Aviation History Research & Publishing 21

Chapter Two - Clash over Trieste

The American media reported on the explosive events almost immediately after the shooting down of the C-47 Skytrain cargo plane. Yugoslav aggression was primarily directed at the American, British, and Italian troops in northern Italy. The contested area, roughly the Venezia-Giulia district, was claimed by Yugoslavia, leading to numerous skirmishes and escalating tensions. Not unjustifiably, Washington feared the worst. The British could deploy 70,000 troops and over a hundred combat aircraft. In contrast, the American Army had only 34,000 troops, and USAFE had no combat air unit stationed in Italy. The Italian Army comprised 122,500 troops and 64,000 carabinieri, but had no tanks or modern equipment. The air force consisted of about 200 obsolete aircraft. Poorly trained, the Italian soldiers needed higher morale. The Yugoslav Army was quite capable of overrunning the Venezia-Giulia district. However, with Russian help, they could succeed in invading all of Italy. The U.S. Joint War Plans Committee estimated that the Red Army could lead fifteen divisions through the Brenner Pass within thirty days of a Yugoslav invasion of northern Italy. Without the Western Alies being able to intervene, Yugo-Russian forces would advance to Calabria in weeks.

Diplomatic crisis

The danger became a reality on August 9, when two Yugoslav Yak-3 fighters from the 254th Fighter Aviation Regiment opened fire on a C-47A of 305th Troop Carrier Squadron and forced it to land in a field close to Kranj near the border between Slovenia and Austria. According to American reports, a navigational error took the C-47 en route to the Udine air base in Italy off course and over Yugoslav territory. When they made contact with the C-47, the Yugoslav fighters claimed that the American intruder was circling the military airfield of Laibach (today Ljubljana).[24]

Onboard were four American crewmembers (including William Crombie, the pilot) and six passengers—three Americans, two Hungarians, and one Turkish officer. Everybody on board survived and was taken prisoner by the Yugoslav Army. The incident triggered a diplomatic crisis between the U.S. and Yugoslavia, soon approaching boiling point. The occasion was another clash between the two nations' armed forces ten days later. Coincidentally, it was another ATC C-47 that was flying over Yugoslav territory because of a navigational error. This time the C-47 again of the 305th Troop Carrier Squadron was shot down by two Yakolev Yak-3 fighters that scrambled from Lesce airfield near Radmannsdorf (today Radovljica) in Slovenia.

An eyewitness in the Slovenian village Bohinjska Bistrica told Associated Press he saw a large transport flying in a southwestern direction. On August 19, 1946, two fighter planes approached the transport plane and shot it down. The witness saw the plane spiraling down in a column of smoke. Two parachutes were spotted. Parachutes and the C-47 went down in the Julian Alps near Bled, south of Klagenfurt, Austria, just two miles inside of Yugoslavia. All five American crew members died in the crash.

Crossing the line

The United States and Great Britain delivered sharp notes to the Yugoslav Government. In the most incentiary-words release, the State Department took the opportunity to accuse the Yugoslav Government of making illegal troop forays into American occupied zone (Zone A) of Trieste in July and of unprovoked attacks on American troops. Yugoslavia claimed the area of the Istrian peninsula, including the city of Trieste, as rightfully hers. And Yugoslav forces regularly crossed the so-called Morgan Line, named after the British General Sir William Duthie Morgan, the Supreme Allied Commander, Mediterranean Theater, that separated Italy and Yugoslavia. Facing each other at this line was a small Anglo-American force of 50,000 troops and only 175 operational fighter aircraft available on the American side[25] and a substantial Yugoslav force of an estimated 150,000 seasoned and Russian-trained troops, 1000 airplanes, and thousands of tanks, trucks, and armored vehicles, the majority provided by the U.S. under lend-lease. There was severe fear that Tito, with the help of Russia, would take over Trieste by force. And that would mean a new war in Europe.

Flashpoint Trieste

The Soviets had brought Yugoslavia under their influence. Partisan-Communist and political leader Marshall Josip Broz Tito was known as a stooge of Jozef Stalin. For many years, there had been friction between Yugoslavia and Italy about the northeastern part of Italy known as the Venezia-Giulia district, particularly about the harbor of Trieste. Stalin demanded Tito's claim to control the harbor and the city of Trieste. It would give the Russians a crucial Mediterranean seaport. From Trieste, commerce would reach Hungary, Czechoslovakia, Poland, the Danube valley, and Romania—all under the influence of the Soviet Union. Not surprisingly, the Russian foreign minister Molotov insisted that Trieste become part of Yugoslavia.

Russia's demand was vigorously resisted by Britain, the United States, and France. To lend a hand to diplomacy and as a warning, Washington sent Vice Admiral Bernhard H. Bieri, the commander of the U.S. Sixth Fleet in the Mediterranean, to Trieste. He was aboard the 10,000-ton cruiser USS Fargo, the flagship of a three-ship detachment that included the destroyers USS Small and USS Power. The British were present in Trieste with a cruiser, a destroyer, a frigate, and a tank-landing ship. This all happened end of June 1946, when 10,000 men of the 88th Blue Devils U.S. infantry division deployed to Gorizia as reinforcements at the Morgan Line.

To add to the pressure, the U.S. Navy sent the impressive aircraft carrier USS Franklin D. Roosevelt to Napels. It was in the Mediterranean on a "goodwill" tour by the U.S. Sixth Fleet and moored on the 27th of August 1946 in the Bay of Naples along with the cruiser USS Little Rock and the destroyers USS New, USS Cone, and USS Corry. Together they formed Carrier Air Group 75, that in September 1946, headed for Pireaus outside Athens to support pro-Western forces that the Communists opposed in the ongoing civil war in Greece. Before docking at Naples, the carrier's full complement of Corsair, Avenger, and Hellcat aircraft, was launched and flew to Capodichino Air Base, were they remained until the carrier group departed.[26]

Cold War begins

The 70 miles (112 kilometers) demarcation line between the Allied-occupied Zone A and Zone B occupied by the Yugoslav Army ran from the Kranjska Gora at the Austrian border to Koper, south of Trieste at the Adriatic Sea. At the same time, Tito charged the United States with spying over Yugoslav territory. He also complained that between July 16 and August 8, the Yugoslav Air Force counted no less than 172 clandestine flights over the northwestern part of Yugoslavia, called Zone B, of Venezia Giulia between Italy, Austria, and Yugoslavia.[27]

Records of the American authorities in Austria and Italy showed that only 74 flights had taken place between those dates and that crews operating the planes had been thoroughly briefed on approved routes avoiding Yugoslavia. The shooting down was the first violent incident between an allied country and a Communist country since the end of World War II. Perhaps it even marked the beginning of the Cold War between East and West.

SIX SUPERFORTS ON FLIGHT FROM U. S. TO REICH

'Atom Bomb' Planes Hop From Florida

WASHINGTON, Nov. 15.—(AP)—Six Army Superfortresses are en route to the American occupied zone of Germany on a "routine" training flight, the Army Air Forces announced today.

Lt. Gen. Ira C. Eaker, deputy commander, said the B-29s would follow the normal Air Transport Command route to Europe, would not travel in formation and would return in about a week.

The flight started from Morrison Field, Florida, but the AAF did not disclose when it began.

There was no elaboration of General Eaker's bare announcement but it was recalled that General Spaatz, Air Forces commander, has said it is planned to replace the smaller B-17 bombers now assigned to the occupation forces with B-29's of the type which dropped the atom bombs on Hiroshima and Nagasaki.

Officials said the flight had no connection with the cancelled plan to send B-29s around the world.

Eaker Announcement

Eaker's announcement said:

"Six Boeing B-29 Superfortresses and two Douglas C-54 Sky Masters are en route to Frankfurt, Germany. The planes are leaving from Morrison Field, Florida, and will fly the regular ATC route to Europe.

"The bombers will not fly in formation. The flight is a routine mission and will acquaint the air personnel with the operating and airport conditions in Europe as well as familiarizing Air Forces ground crews in Europe with the characteristics and maintenance techniques of Boeing B-29s.

"The bombers will be supported by two Douglas C-54's carrying spare parts and trained technicians. The bombers will remain about one week before returning to the United States.

"Further details will be announced by the commanding general, United States forces in the European Theater."

The U.S. responded to the tense developments in Europe by sending six heavy Boeing B-29 Stratofortresses on a training mission to Rhein-Main Air Base near Frankfurt, Germany. These bombers were from the 43rd Bombardment Group at Morrison Field in Florida and made a stopover at Lajes Air Base, Azores. It was primarily an attempt to impress the Soviets, which had to cave in. The B-29s were standard A-types unsuitable for dropping atomic weapons. The B-29s flew along the border of Soviet-occupied territory, visited the capitals of several free-European countries, and surveyed numerous airfields for possible use by B-29s. While the flight could not be regarded as a direct threat to Russia, the presence of B-29s and their reputation as carriers of the A-bomb served notice that the U.S. was not abandoning Western Europe to the Communists. In early December 1946, the flight returned home.

Chapter Two - Clash over Trieste

In 1946, USAFE began collecting electronic intelligence (ELINT) on Soviet activities. Two former Boeing B-17 bombers in the Casey Jones photo mapping project (1945-1946) were equipped with ELINT gear. Soon, more B-17s joined them for photo purposes. One such Fortress was the mysterious F-9 44-85541. This B-17G was modified to F-9C photo reconnaissance standards at the Wright Aircraft Factory modernization center on Louisville Air Base, Kentucky. In April 1945, this F-9 came to the 8th Air Force in Europe. But it is unclear to which unit it was assigned. It turned up in 1947, with about 20 B-17s assigned to the 10th Headquarters and Base Services Squadron at Oberpfaffenhofen Air Base near Munich in Germany. Most of these B-17s moved to nearby Fürstenfeldbruck Air Base the following year. But 44-85541 "disappeared." Similar all-black RB-17Gs turned up in the Middle East and Taiwan; one, with serial 44-85531, with '531' on the tail. According to its Individual Aircraft Record Card, the B-17 was transferred to an organization outside the USAF on 4 February 1953 for a top secret assignment. The Fortress was likely part of the Republic of China Air Force's 34th Black Bat Squadron. Since 1953, the 34th operated all-black Boeing RB-17s and Douglas RB-26s in tightly secret CIA-organized missions out of Hsinchu Air Base over the Chinese mainland to conduct various covert operations. In 1956, they began conducting electronic reconnaissance, psychological warfare (leaflet droppings), and agent airdrop missions in China's Northeast, as far west as Gansu, Qinghai, and Yunnan provinces, and as far south as Thailand, Myanmar, and Laos. 1957 the RB-17s were replaced by heavily modernized Lockheed P-2V Neptune maritime patrol and anti-submarine warfare planes. Redesignated RB-69s, the CIA, in the spring of 1957, deployed two of these planes to Wiesbaden Air Base in Germany, where they were attached to the resident 7405th Support Squadron. The CIA used these planes for covert ELINT-mission. Details of these clandestine, paramilitary CIA operations remain classified.

For the United States, Zone A and free access from Austria through the Po Valley to the strategically located port city of Trieste was of great importance and had everything to do with the particular position of Austria after the German Reich.

Soviet aggression and U.S. war plans

Indeed, Austria's fate after 1945 differed from Germany's. Austria, which Hitler's Third Reich annexed in 1938, was just like Germany, divided into four zones of occupation after the German capitalization. There was a Soviet zone in the east, an American zone west of it, and a French zone in the Tyrol and Vorarlberg.

The British zone covered the southern provinces of Styria and Carinthia. Vienna, the capital city, was divided into four allied sectors, just like Berlin. The Western Allies had to prepare for two contingencies in Austria. The most important one was for the event of a third world war, and the second one was for any Communist aggression and their attempts to take control in the eastern provinces and Vienna, similar to what was developing in Eastern Germany and Berlin.

That was the atmosphere surrounding the late forties in Vienna. However, the likelihood of wholesale Soviet aggression into Western Europe, which would plunge the world into a new global war, was very remote. But if the Soviets would attack in force, the United States and its Western Allies were, with the massive demobilization after the Nazi defeat, much too weak to make a stand in Europe. The U.S. Air War Plans Division in 1946 posited a Soviet invasion of Europe. The scenario with codename Pincher was that the Western Allies in Western Germany, vastly outnumbered, would retreat to the river Rhine and then offer whatever resistance they could muster.

Overrunning Europe

In anticipation, the U.S. strategy forsaw that the Red Army would overrun most of the European continent, and allied forces would depart from French and, via Austria, from Italian seaports, similar to the retreat of the British Army in Dunkirk in 1940. Once American troops retreated from continental Europe—and left their air bases in Britain, possibly Spain, and North Africa, as well as in Asia and the Pacific— they would conduct a strategic air campaign, using nuclear weapons to force the Soviet Union to collapse.

In this geopolitical scenario, the port of Trieste held vital strategic significance, making a territorial dispute with Yugoslavia a potential flashpoint for a new war between the Western Allies and Lenin's Communists.

Pressure on Tito

Fortunately, it didn't get that far. Knowing that U.S. President Harry Truman had the atomic bomb in his back pocket, Joseph Stalin didn't push the emerging crisis to the limit. He pressured his Communist ally Tito to such an extent that the latter gave in. The ultimatum issued by the U.S.—release of the crew of the C-47 that force landed at Kranj, repatriation of the killed crew members of the C-47 that the Yugoslav Air Force shot down at Bled, payments for the two airplanes and suffering caused, and a ban on attacking American planes—was accepted by Stalin under pressure. This knee-jerk reaction was also the immediate initiation of the split between the two Communist leaders, the move by the Soviet leader that contributed to Yugoslavia drifting away from Moscow.

In 1948, Tito openly broke with Stalin, though he continued to proclaim his allegiance to the Communist ideology. During the Cold War, Yugoslavia hovered between Eastern and Western alliances. Tito was regarded as much an ally as an enemy.

Covert B-17 flights

Likely USAFE used the Casey Jones photomapping program as a cover-up for reconnaissance missions along the demarcation line between Italy and Yugoslavia and covert flights over Yugoslav territory. In April 1946, USAFE flew thirty-two such Ferret missions.[28] Several ELINT B-17s from the secretive Detachment A of 10th Photo Reconnaissance Group operating out of Fürth Airfield, near Nürnberg in Germany, were used for reconnaissance flights along the Morgan Line[29]—and even perhaps over Slovenia.

However, Secretary of State William L. Clayton firmly denied such violation of Yugoslav airspace. On September 3, 1946, in a note to Tito, he confirmed that from July 16, U.S. B-17s armed and unarmed bombers made regular flights from Vienna to Udine, patrolling along the Morgan line.[30] They tested the Yugoslav reaction, and at least two unarmed B-17s were on ELINT missions on August 28. They were to gather electronic information to find out how the Yugoslav Air Force could monitor Allied aircraft movements and intercept strayed aircraft even under bad weather conditions. It turned out that the Yugoslav Air Force was effectively using radar equipment left behind at various locations by the Luftnachrichten-Regiment 248 of the German Luftwaffe. The German air defense during World War II used state-of-the-art radar systems for detecting and intercepting enemy aircraft. Long-range early warning detection was done with radar systems code-named Mammut, Wassermann, and Jagdschloss. In contrast, the technologically advanced Würzburg radar built by Telefunken was the cornerstone of the Luftwaffe's ground-controlled interception. Thanks to the German radars, the Yugoslav Air Force could keep an eye on the entire crisis area around the Morgan line and steer their Yak-3 fighter planes flawlessly to any border violators.

Washington flexes its muscles

The Kremlin cared little about American nuclear hegemony, probably knowing that they too would soon have such a weapon of mass destruction at their disposal. The U.S. military leadership had little choice but to flex its superior technological muscle. Thus, B-29s were sent on world tours to demonstrate the U.S. global reach capability. Col. Clarence S. Irvine's trans-polar flight in a B-29 called Pacusan Dreamboat from Honolulu to Cairo in Egypt was much publicized.

On October 4, 1946, he took off and mastered the 9,500 miles (16,576 kilometers) nonstop, flying over the Artic in 39 hours and 36 minutes. Flying the same B-29, Irvine set the transcontinental speed record to 450 mph (724 km/h) in December 1945. He covered the 2,464 miles' distance (3,965 kilometers) between Long Beach, California, and Washington, D.C., in 5 hours and 17 minutes. The remarkable achievement was surpassed on January 27, 1946, by Col. William H. Councill, who flew a modified Lockheed P-80R 44-85123 nonstop across the U.S. to make the first

In 1946, the U.S. Atomic Strike Force became a reality as part of the new Strategic Air Command. WWII legend General Carl Andrew, nicknamed "Tooey" Spaatz (1891 - 1974), defined its mission: "The command will be prepared to conduct long-range offensive operations in any part of the world either independently or in cooperation with land and naval forces; to conduct maximum range reconnaissance over land or sea either independently or in cooperation with naval forces; to provide combat units capable of intense and sustained combat operations employing the latest and most advanced weapons; to train units and personnel for the maintenance of the Strategic Forces in all parts of the world; to perform such missions as the Commanding General, Army Air Forces, may direct."
The next step for Spaatz was the formation of an independent air force operating alongside the U.S. Army and the U.S. Navy. This happened a year later, on September 18, 1947, when the Chiefs of Staff deleted the word "Army" from the U.S. Army Air Force: the United States Air Force (USAF) as an independent service was born. Photo: U.S. Air Force.

Chapter Two - **Clash over Trieste**

P-80 jet fighters to Europe

By the time the Russians started developing their first jet fighters, the British Gloster Meteor and the American Lockheed P-80 Shooting Star were already operational in considerable numbers. In the spring of 1946, around three hundred P-80s were operational with the USAAF. The straight-winged P-80 was hastily developed by Lockheed's mastermind Kelly Johnson, who led the famous Skunk Works, the name for Lockheed's Advanced Development Projects. Lockheed started designing and building the P-80 in 1943 (in only 143 days!). The XP-80 first flew on January 8, 1944, and as early as November 1944, the U.S. War Department in Washington had decided to send four Lockheed YP-80 test versions to the European battlefield for operational testing. They were shipped from New York in crates to England and Italy. Two arrived at RAF Burtonwood, Lancashire, in late December. The two YP-80s destined for testing in Italy arrived at Lesina Air Base (Foggia complex) in late January 1945. Testing of the four YP-80s, conducted under the code name Extraversion, was fraught with mystery. The jets were maintained by Lockheed civilian personnel and flown by military pilots. In the spring of 1946, around 300 P-80 Shooting Stars were operational with the USAAF. The majority were stationed in the U.S., but a number of these jets were to be based in Germany. The War Department allocated thirty-two P-80 jets to USAFE. These jets augmented two fighter groups in Germany that operated the remaining Republic P-47Ds and P-51Ds of the USAAF. USAFE assigned the P-80s to the 31st Fighter Group at Giebelstadt Air Base. In September/October 1946, the P-80s were transferred to nearby Kitzingen Air Base (Giebelstadt was to become a B-29 base) and flight operations continued from this new base. One major problem was that Western European climate corroded the sensitive General Electric/Allison J33 turbojet engine which consequently had to be replaced frequently. In addition, a number of P-80s crashed during the European evaluation flights - the P-80's loss figures were the highest in the USAAF. Between March and September 1946, thirty-six aircraft were lost. The figures in Europe were equally high. Lack of replacement engines and high losses, led to the P-80s of the 31ste FG being withdrawn from European operation. A year later the P-80, then in better shape, would make its return.

The partially dismantled aircraft were shipped to Bremerhaven, loaded on barges, and floated up the Weser River to Bremen. Without the tail section, Jeeps provisionally towed them through the city center to the nearby airfield, where the 30th Mobile Repair Squadron assembled them. After assembly, the P-80s were flown to Nordholz Air Base to calibrate instruments before departing for Giebelstadt Air Base.
Photo: UNITC-Medienvertrieb/Germany.

One of the most famous aircraft of all time! The simple MiG-15 jet fighter (the Western name is "Fagot") was built in higher numbers than any other post-war aircraft. It is estimated that more than 18,000 MiG-15s, in various versions, have been built in factories in Russia, Czechoslovakia, Poland, and China. It has served in the air forces of at least 44 countries and played a significant role in the Korean War against U.S. North American F-86 Sabres. Under the terms of a curious Anglo-Russian trade agreement, the UK agreed to export Rolls-Royce Nene Mk. I and Mk. II turbojet engines. The British engine was reverse-engineered by Vladimir Yakovlevich Klimov and manufactured at Factory No. 45 in Moscow as the RD-45F. The engine produced a maximum of 22.26 kilonewtons of thrust (5,004 pounds). Most MiG-15s used this engine, giving the fighter a top speed of 652 mph (1,050 km/h) and a service ceiling of 49,869 feet (15.2 kilometers). Source: Aircraft of the Soviet Union. Photo: Mikoyan Design Bureau.

transcontinental jet flight. He completed the 2,457 miles (3,954 kilometers) distance between Daugherty Field, Long Beach, and LaGuardia Airport, New York, in only 4 hours, 13 minutes, and 26 seconds at an average speed of 584 mph (940 km/h). In all, during 1946, the U.S. Army Air Force put twenty-seven official aviation records in the books of the Fédération Aéronautique Internationale, primarily achieved with B-29s for payloads, endurance, speed, altitudes, and any combination of these.

Progress in Russia too

Technologically, Russia was still well behind the West, and the U.S. was only too happy to play that card simply by showing that it was ahead on many fronts. Especially in jet propulsion, the U.S. had a significant advantage over its Russian rival. However, the British laid the foundation for the modern jet age with their Rolls Royce Nene engine. This centrifugal compressor turbojet delivered 5,000 pounds of thrust, double what BMW's German Jumo engine gave. The Jumo powered the Messerschmitt Me-262 of the Luftwaffe but this jet fighterbomber needed two of them to achieve good performance. Russia took advantage of German jet technology that it had managed to plunder from German development centers. With the assistance of German engineers, Russian developers successfully produced production-ready gas turbines based on German technology for Mikoyan and Gurevich's MiG-9 and Yakovlev's Yak-15. It was during this time that the development of one of the most famous aircraft of all time began.

The Model S with prototype number I-310 was a simple design by the Mikoyan-Gurevich (MiG) Design Bureau based on German studies. It had a swept wing and a large T-tail. Western intelligence would soon write thick reports about the Red Army's cold war trump card: the MiG-15. The design of the MiG started in March 1946. In a meeting, the Kremlin issued the requirements to all constructors charged with the design. The Red Army needed a swept-wing, high-altitude day interceptor able to operate from rough airstrips that could reach a speed of 0.9 Mach. And production should start no later than the end of 1948.

Chapter Three
Global capability

The Consolidated-Vultee Aircraft Corporation (Convair) XB-36 (42-13570) made its maiden flight on August 8, 1946. The bomber was built to carry up to 86,000 pounds (39,000 kilograms) of conventional bombs in a four-section bomb bay. It could carry two 43,600-pound (19,777 kilograms) T-12 conventional explosive earth-penetrating bombs. When armed with nuclear weapons, the B-36 could carry several thermonuclear bombs. By combining the bomb bays, one Mk.17 25-megaton thermonuclear bomb could be carried. The B-36 came into production in 1948 at the Convair plant in Fort Worth, Texas. It was propelled by six mighty Pratt & Whitney R-4360 Wasp 28-cylinder four-row radial piston engines with characteristic pusher propellers and 3,000 horsepower each. Later B-36 models were modernized with even stronger engines and with four additional General Electric J47-GE-19 jet engines mounted in pods on the outer wings. These jet engines added to the speed and service ceiling of the mighty bomber. During the Cold War, 382 B-36s were built in various versions.. Photo: Convair.

In World War II, the bombers of the 8th Air Force made a mark in the eventual victory with long-range strategic bombing missions. It was a tribute to General Billy Mitchell—the creator of strategic bombing—who commanded all American air combat units in France in World War I. Mitchell put his knowledge into practice at the Battle of Saint-Mihiel in September 1918. He ordered a force of 1,481 aircraft from the U.S. Army Air Service and Allied air forces to attack German positions behind the lines in waves. In doing so, he paved the way for ground forces to capture the strategic salient of Saint-Mihiel from the Germans, thereby recapturing, among other things, the vital rail link from Toul to Verdun. The plan succeeded. Until then, planes were mainly used in an "observation" role, the observation of enemy positions in support of artillery. And there were aircraft for pursuit," for local protection of troops on the ground. Mitchell added an important task: "strategic aviation," as he called it. That was everything else—beyond observation and pursuit, a force entirely directed at the enemy air weapon wherever it might be. The goal was gaining air superiority, after which strategic bombers could destroy the enemy ground forces, transportation infrastructure, ammunition depots, communications centers, etc. After World War I, Mitchell became a great promoter of an independent air force alongside the Army and Navy. In Washington, he did not immediately gain a foothold for his ideas. He fought a lonely battle against the established West Point alums, to which he did not belong.

The Air Service, as it was determined in 1920, remained a part of the U.S. Army, working with the U.S. Navy to keep the U.S. safe from enemy invasion. Mitchell's promotion of the aircraft as a strategic weapon was criticized heavily by his colleagues and was even considered insubordination. It cost him his military career; he was court-martialed and dismissed. Only after he died in 1936 was he rehabilitated by President Franklin Roosevelt. His theories on precision strategic bombing became the basis of the doctrine of strategic warfare developed by the Air Corps Tactical School (ACTS). Adherents of the Mitchell doctrine included Ira C. Eaker, Curtis E. Le May, and Carl A. Spaatz, the three individuals who played leading roles in the air offensive against Germany and Japan. Having commanded the U.S. Eighth and Twelfth Air Forces, Carl Spaatz was appointed Major General in January 1944 and given command of the U.S. Strategic Air Forces in Europe. In April 1945, freshly promoted to a four-star General, he was placed in command of the U.S. Strategic Air Forces Pacific, headquartered on the isle of Guam. From there, General Spaatz led the strategic bombing operations of the B-29s, including the two atomic attacks conducted by Major General Le May's Composite Group.

U.S. Strategic Air Command

The atomic weapon gave an entirely new meaning to strategic and drastically revolutionized warfare with their unprecedented destructive power; one atomic bomb of 20 kilotons of TNT—the size of the Nagasaki bomb—had the equivalent destructive power of a fleet of 4,800 fully loaded conventional B-29s. The atomic bombs, however, were large, weighing 10,000 pounds (4.536 kilograms), and could only be delivered by specially modified B-29s. Lt General Ira Eaker, Spaatz's deputy, conducted a study on the atomic weapons deterrence strategy of the Army Air Force. This study laid the foundation of an elite "Atomic Strike Force" equipped with the most advanced aircraft and the best crews, equipment, and training. This strike force would rely on the pioneer 509th with its 22 B-29 Silverplates as a nucleus of an atomic strike capability that would be ready at all times. The other very heavy bomber (VHB) groups were the 40th and the 444th Bombardment Groups,[31] with one squadron in each of these two groups being modified to carry the atomic bomb.[32]

B-29A 44-86385 at RAF Marham in 1947. Until 1948, the stationing of U.S. B-29 heavy bombers on air bases of the RAF in England was politically out of the question. However, the Strategic Air Command did deploy B-29 to bases in England for short periods. In June 1947, after a three-day stay in Germany, several B-29s of the 340th Bombardment Squadron of the 97th Bombardment Group from Smoky Hill, Kansas, arrived at RAF Marham, Norfolk, for a week-long goodwill visit. B-29s had been operating in Europe since the end of World War II. They were occasional visitors, such as B-29A 44-61679 in 1945, or they were part of a deployment, such as sextet B-29s that was based at Rhein-Main in 1946 for a while. Giebelstadt Air Base in Bavaria regularly hosted special ferret F-13/RB-29s in 1947. One was 45-21812, nicknamed Sitting Duck, which operated out of Giebelstadt in September 1947. This ELINT aircraft with specialized radar detection and analysis equipment was deployed to Ladd Field in Alaska from May until August 1947 and explored the northern Siberian coast, the Bering Strait, and the southern Siberian coast along the Kamchatka peninsula, searching for Soviet radars. While stationed in Bavaria, Sitting Duck flew missions along the air corridors to Berlin. The unarmed ferret was then tucked between two armed B-29s that would follow a few miles behind. After its European tour, 45-21812 became part of SAC's first permanent electronic reconnaissance organization. The 324th Radio Countermeasures Squadron initially consisted of the ELINT B-29 and an old B-17, but the unit grew to six RB-29 ferrets by the summer of 1948. Based at McGuire AFB, New Jersey, the 324th provided crews for sorties flown from RAF Mildenhall, England; Rhein-Main, Germany; Yokota, Japan; and Ladd Field, Alaska. Photo: San Diego Air and Space Museum.

Chapter Three - Global capability

The three groups were part of the 58th Bombardment Wing headquartered at March Field, California. In fact, with the 509th at Roswell Field, New Mexico, near Los Alamos, where the atomic bombs were built, the 58th Bombardment Wing formed the basis of Strategic Air Command (SAC), announced by Spaatz in March 1946. The New SAC, along with the two other combat organizations—Tactical Air Command (TAC) and Air Defense Command (ADC)—would be the prelude to an independently operating United States Air Force and, along with the U.S. Navy and U.S. Army, should safeguard the democratic, free West from Communist threats. The SAC embodied the combat groups of the long-range striking forces. The ADC became responsible for the continental United States' air defense and coordinating continental air units into effective fighting forces, including the Air National Guard and the Air Reserve. The TAC would cooperate in missions with the ground forces. The plan was to establish an air force consisting of seventy groups—21 of which would be VHBs—manned by 400,000 personnel and entailing some 14,200 aircraft (8,000 aircraft would be in the regular Air Force, with the other 6,200 going to the National Guard and Air Reserves). Spaatz gained a solid reputation with the American public because of his performance in World War II. He was known as a steadfast and decisive leader, highly knowledgeable, and full of humor, quick and witty.

Consequently, his plans for a new, smaller air force were enthusiastically received, not least by President Truman, who looked primarily to the cost aspect of the plans. As long as the U.S. defense spent little money, it was fine. That frugal attitude of Washington was explainable after the enormous financial efforts of World War II and the recovery of the affected Western economies. But it did have repercussions on the strength of the U.S. military. The air force was hit hard anyway by the hasty demobilization and little was left of the world's most powerful air force. It disappointed the planners working on the Pincher war plan. The new Strategic Air Command needed to provide the approximate battle groups to meet its nuclear objectives. However, with only one combat-ready bombing unit—the 509th Bombardment Group*—SAC could do little. Washington stirred the propaganda drum vigorously to bring out an opposite picture.

B-29s not welcome in Europe

In the weeks following the announcement of the Air Force reorganization, there were reports, directed or not by Washington, of an imminent rebuilding of the USAF organization in Europe. The Associated Press reported in April 1946—quoting anonymous American military sources in Europe—that by the summer of 1946, USAFE could already count on more than 70,000 highly trained men. Reportedly, SAC moved as many as two hundred B-29s to England; another three hundred were on their way. Four airfields in France were prepared for the B-29s, with another four more in Germany.

Furthermore, the fast, twin-engine Douglas A-26 Invader light attack bomber would have been shipped to Germany in large numbers, as would large shipments of Lockheed

---

* Before June 10, 1947 known as 509th Composite Group.

Little Boy on the hydraulic lift in the atomic loading pit readied for loading in the bomb bay of B-29A 44-86292 Enola Gay. The photograph was taken at North Field Air Base on Tinian Island in preparation for the bombing of Hiroshima on August 6, 1945. The bomber bases in England and Germany lacked such pits, which made strategic nuclear operations in Europe difficult or even impossible. Photo: NARA.

P-80s that would be the nucleus of a fighter force. These fighters were assembled upon arrival in Bremen and prepared for deployment from German bases. Only the latter—the arrival of the P-80 in Germany—was true; the rest was false information.

Not wonderful

As early as mid-1945, the planners in Washington had anticipated deploying five groups of B-29 Stratofortresses to Europe in a project called Wonderful. Initially, the B-29 was not intended for operations in Europe at all. The heavy bomber, with its mighty bombload and impressive range, was meant to deploy to the Pacific and fight the war against Japan. Its larger combat range than that of the B-17 bomber made the B-29 ideally suited to reach the Japanese mainland from islands in the Pacific. In Europe, the B-29's combat range was not a strategic advantage; B-17s and B-24s could reach all enemy targets from bases in England, which they have done since 1942. In contrast, the B-29's operational flight ceiling was a significant disadvantage on the European battlefield. The heavy B-29 had a service ceiling of 31,850 ft (9,710 m), which was quite a bit lower than that of the B-17, which had an operational flying altitude of 35,600 ft (10,850 m). The B-29 thus flew 3,750 feet lower than a B-17, which would make the heavy bomber easy prey for German radar-guided flak and supercharged Fw190 Luftwaffe fighters. These fast and heavily armed interceptors had a magnificent service ceiling of 33,960 ft (10,350 m). Washington sent a single B-29 to the U.S. Eighth Air Force in England during the war in Europe. In March 1944, YB-29A serial No. 41-36393, nicknamed Hobo Queen, was in England under the guise of a series of evaluation flights. Its presence in the European War Theater was more a show of force along several U.S. units at RAF airfields such as St. Mawgan, in Cornwall, RAF Horsham, RAF Bassingbourn, RAF Knettishall, and RAF Glatton. After much promotion and crowded displays, Hobo Queen left RAF St. Mawgan for RAF Kharagpur, India, on April 2 that year. After the war, there was much discussion about whether the B-29 was also operationally used against the Nazis. It wasn't. There had never been a B-29 over the European continent during the war.

Under Operation Wonderful, B-29s were scheduled to begin moving as early as September 1945. Almost immediately, however, demobilization chaos imposed reality; the deployments were delayed and postponed several times. In January 1946, Wonderful was postponed until the summer. The new SAC couldn't handle the planned deployment, and at the same time, the B-29's reputation as an atomic bomber played tricks on the planners. Politics in former Allies France and Britain turned against nuclear weapons on their territory, undoubtedly motivated by fear of the Red Army's reaction and the knowledge that the Soviets were as strong as ever and barely engaged in demobilization. Moreover, they were right around the corner. Politics kept the planners busy, and in the spring of 1947, Spaatz stated that sovereignty sensibilities would curtail the scope and scale of American deployments. American B-29s were not welcome in countries like England, France, the Netherlands, Denmark, or Norway. Their reputation as nuclear bombers made them politically undesirable. The U.S. could sta-

*This bomber in Boeing's Fortress series was the successor to the B-29, which was a further development. The B-50, of which 370 were built in various versions, formed the backbone of the Strategic Air Command's nuclear deterrence fleet from 1948 to 1955. Designated initially as the B-29D, the B-50 was essentially an improved version of the B-29. However, a large number of modifications caused its re-designation as the B-50. The B-50 had more powerful Pratt & Whitney radial engines than the B-29, a more robust structure, a taller fin, and other improvements, such as a pressurized cockpit. It flew faster and higher than the B-29 and, fitted with two 700-US-gallon (2,650 liters) external tanks, it had a ferry range of 7,750 miles (12,470 kilometers). Boeing B-50D 48-096 above was converted to EB-50D as the mothership for the Bell X-2 rocket plane research program in 1953.
Photo: U.S. Air Force.*

tion its B-29s in occupied countries—Germany, Austria, Italy, and the Pacific—because the capitulated countries had no say in that. In Italy, Foggia in particular, the U.S. could still expand and make the bases suitable for atomic use, but the German bases presented their problems. The new Allied commander in Germany, General Joseph McNarney, who already did not foresee a large occupation air force, also saw no role for B-29s in the occupation force. Moreover, he feared bomber airfields would be vulnerable to Soviet air attacks. Besides, he did not have the ground forces to protect them. In May 1946, the AAF canceled Wonderful. Not much more of the once-mighty U.S. Air Force was left than a dog barking with its mouth shut.

Propaganda and pure bluff

What was left to the AAF was little more than to maintain a few groups with obsolete B-17s in Europe. These were not remotely capable of deploying atomic bombs—the B-17 could not carry, let alone eject, the 10,000-pound Little Boy. Henceforth, B-29s would be deployed into Germany periodically for training and familiarization purposes, as it was officially called. This would ease the concern of European countries over their safety. It also lowered distress among Europeans regarding the bombers that had flattened Hiroshima and Nagasaki not being permanently based within their midst. In fact, the B-29s sent to Europe could not be used for atomic tasks at all. The types that the AAF deployed to Germany weren't modernized to deliver nuclear bombs. And—besides Foggia in Italy—none of the bases were equipped for it. It was all one big theater of disinformation, propaganda, and bluff. Or perhaps not?

Serious rhetoric

Was it all bluff that Washington came up with, or did the Soviet Union really have to take the rhetoric seriously? What is certain is that the German air base Rhein-Main, where Strategic Air Command had stationed six more Boeing B29s for a week in 1946 by way of training, received a thorough overhaul in 1947. The large air base—just about the largest base of the Luftwaffe during the war—had suffered substantial damage from numerous Allied bombing raids. Especially in the last year of the war, the air base of Jagdgeschwader 4, among others, suffered severely. A devastating bombardment by 109 Boeing B-17 Flying Fortresses of the Eighth Air Force from England on March 22, 1945, put the base out of action. Because of the rapidly advancing forces of General George Patton's U.S. Third Army, the Wehrmacht evacuated the air base and blew up all remaining infrastructure. Immediately after the American capture of the air base, the U.S. prepared it to serve as a transport base for the U.S. occupation forces in Germany and to host Strategic Air Command's heavy Boeing B-29 Superfortresses. Responsible for the rehabilitation of the air base was the USAFE Air Engineer Section. The runway was extended to 6,000 feet (1,829 meters) in 1946, and a system of taxiways connected dozens of dispersals at the base. In October, the Air Engineer Section employed 2,500 men on the project, making it the largest construction project in the U.S. zone of occupation.[33] Similar work had taken place at suitable bomber air bases throughout Europe. The Air Engineer Section rehabilitated or built thirty-three air bases in the U.S. zone of occupation in Germany alone. The section reinforced runways, taxiways, and dispersal areas, modified infrastructure, and built ammunition bunkers. All that was still missing were the atomic bombs.

Global capability

It had to impress the Soviets and show that the U.S. Air Force could fly groups of mission-ready bombers anytime, anywhere across the Atlantic, bringing them within shooting distance, so to speak, of the Soviet-dominated Eastern Bloc. And to further rub the global capabilities of Strategic Air Command into the Russians, the Americans organized one show of force after another, whether it was setting long-range records or the first flight of the mighty

Convair B-36 strategic bomber, cynically named the Peacemaker. With a wingspan of 230 ft (70 m) and a length of 162 feet (49.40 meters), the aircraft was designed to deliver bombs weighing up to 86,000 lbs (39,009 kilograms), but early models had to be modernized under the Saddletree program (successor of Silverplate) of the Air Material Command to carry and deliver atomic bombs. Its combat range was 4,000 miles (6,437 kilometers), but the B-36 could cover 10,000 miles (16,000 kilometers) nonstop without payload. And by the way, the B-36 flew 435 mph (700 km/h), and the service ceiling was 43,600 ft (13,300 m).

Those were not bad ratings for the time. That had to impress the Russians, who had gotten no further than copying the Boeing B-29 of which they managed to acquire four examples. These were aircraft with which crews had made emergency landings on Russian territory during the war in Asia. The Tupolev Tu-4, given life in 1949, had been created based on reverse engineering. The Russians carefully disassembled the interned B-29s and then copied them almost exactly. With the Tu-4, the Russian copycats had their bomber capable of dropping an atomic bomb. The next item on their armament list was a nuclear bomb.

Why would Russia worry?

With the Russian Tu-4 long-range bombers developed and in production in the Tupolev factory in Moscow, MiG jet fighters being produced in vast numbers, the development atomic bomb progressing, and with over 200 divisions available—of which fifteen with more than 350,000 troops in their occupied zone in Germany—what would worry Russia? Stalin was not a man who the U.S. could intimidate. He wasn't intimidated in Potsdam when Truman

Boeing B-29A 44-61822 was converted to F-13 standard (photoreconnaissance). In 1946, it took part in the Crossroads nuclear tests. Nicknamed "Belle of Bikini," it was, together with seven other F-13s and two C-54s, part of Task Unit 1.5.2., an Army Air Photographic Unit that conducted photographic air operations and furnished aircraft for radiological reconnaissance flights. During the nuclear tests, it was stationed on Kwajalein Atoll. The photograph shows the F-13 as RB-29A from the 16th Photographic Reconnaissance Squadron of the 91st Strategic Reconnaissance Group/311th Air Division, the primary reconnaissance organization of the Strategic Air Command. The picture was taken at Fürstenfeldbruck Air Base. In the spring of 1948, the RB-29 was relocated to the German air base when tension between East and West over Berlin increased. Photo: U.S. Air Force.

Chapter Three - Global capability

Another RB-29A at Fürstenfeldbruck Air Base, Germany. After a reconnaissance mission, the B-29 is parked at its hard stand while the ground crew is waiting to start servicing the plane. According to the caption of this USAF photo taken in May 1948, it is a photoreconnaissance RB-29 from the 16th Photographic Reconnaissance Squadron. The B-29 training deployments to Fürstenfeldbruck were each supported by two C-54 transport aircraft of the 1st Air Transport Unit and one RB-29 (F-13) aircraft of the 16th Reconnaissance Squadron from the 91st Strategic Reconnaissance Group, McGuire AFB, NJ. Later in 1948, this group had six RB-29s deployed to the UK. Until the early 1950s, small detachments of SAC RB-29s were continually rotated to forward bomber bases in Europe and Asia. Photo: U.S. Air Force.

told him about the Alamogordo nuclear explosion and he was not intimidated by the B-29s of the U.S. Strategic Air Force that were used to demonstrate worldwide reach and deterrence. Why not?

Perhaps the Russians were aware of the actual situation. The U.S. nuclear deterrent at the beginning of the Cold War can best be described as confusing. Permanently stationing a nuclear B-29 strike force in Europe proved impossible. It could be in Germany, but the airfields were vulnerable to the Russian troops standing at relatively close range. In England, General Carl Spaatz and English Air Chief Marshal Sir Arthur Tedder reached an agreement in secrecy in July 1946 about the Americans' use of the RAF airfields Lakenheath and Sculthorpe.[34] But work to prepare these airfields for the arrival of B-29 Silverplates and to support atomic operations became publicly known as Project Barbara. After the secret plans were leaked via the Washington Post[35] in the fall of 1946 and categorically denied by President Truman, the project fell short of completion. Two years later, under pressure from increased tensions, Project Barbara would still be completed, and it was in the early 1950s that fully assembled bombs could finally be shipped to Britain and many more bases in England.

And then there was the American nuclear stockpile that in 1946 amounted to nine atomic bombs. That is to say: material for nine atomic Mark III Fat Man bombs was available. When Truman was informed of this tiny number by Eisenhower, he promptly scrapped the planned third Bikini nuclear test under the Crossroad program. Apparently, Truman thought that the one bomb made the difference and that a new war could be won with a stockpile of seven bombs. The reality is that the initial war plan of the Joint War Plans Committee from 1946 called for 196 atomic bombs needed for nuclear offensive measures against industrial targets in the Soviet Union. The U.S. had nowhere near that

On the Edge

number in 1947 and it would be at least three years before the U.S. had anything approaching the number of 196.[36] Adding to the Pentagon's problem was the Silverplate B-29, or to be precise, the lack of them.

B-29 training deployments to Europe

The U.S. Strategic Air Command did not permanently station B-29s in Europe but deployed them on a rotational basis; each time, a different unit was going on a so-called training deployment. Early in 1947, the Air Staff approved plans for regular rotations. First, squadrons of B-29s were sent, and later also entire groups of sixty B-29s. In June 1947, nine B-29s of the 340th Bombardment Squadron of the 97th Bombardment Group deployed from Smoky Hill, Kansas, to Giebelstadt, Germany. They arrived on June 5 after a 7,500 miles (12,070 kilometers) transatlantic flight with a stopover on Lajes Air Base, Azores. After a three-day stay in Germany—during which the B-29s did formation flying over Berlin[37]—the B-29s departed for RAF Marham for a weeklong goodwill visit. This visit was in return of RAF No. 35 Squadron, which with its sixteen Lancaster bombers, toured the USA in the summer of 1946.

The 340th Squadron returned home only to turn around and head once again for Germany, this time with the rest of the 97th Group. The group's two-week deployment that July included flights to several cities, although visits to Copenhagen and Paris were canceled for diplomatic reasons. A meeting on the Marshall Plan was opening in Paris, and it was felt not such a good idea to have B-29s landing at Orly or Le Bourget. Because of Soviet objections, the B-29s that visited Berlin did not fly in formation but paid single flyover visits to Berlin. The 97th returned home again on July 19. Through the middle of September, three other groups made short trips to Europe, making training flights as far afield as Italy and the south shore of the Mediterranean. Eventually, Headquarters SAC objected that these operations were interfering with training, and eventually, they were stopped. In their place came squadron-sized, thirty-day missions in November and December, with units of the 28th and 307th Bombardment Groups participating. For the latter, the overseas base shifted to Fürstenfeldbruck, which had better facilities than Giebelstadt—and it was rumored that it also boasted a much better mess hall. The results of these first visits of B-29s to Europe were encouraging. Missions were flown along the Russian sector borders, and the bombers paid visits to bases in England, France, Turkey, and Greece, the latter for flag-showing missions along the Bulgarian border, to impress the Communist guerillas united in the Greek People's Liberation Army. As part of navigational flight training, the Germany-African-Middle East route was popular because it provided good all-terrain, all-weather practice. The 3,600-mile (5,794 kilometers) run from Fürstenfeldbruck to Dhahran in Saudi Arabia was popular and almost daily. Rotations gave units an excellent opportunity to deploy under simulated combat conditions, and to keep SAC's mobility plans up-to-date. It was a permanent demonstration of USAF to reach far and able to operate everywhere on the globe.

SAC's different story in Asia

The SAC B-29s remained regular visitors

In 1947, the USAF started to show that it was slowly recovering from demobilization. SAC units flew many simulated attacks on major metropolitan areas in the U.S. Large formations of B-29s theoretically bombed cities such as Los Angeles (April 11), New York (May 16), and Chicago (August 1). The most significant raid was on May 16, known as Operation Pacific. In a maximum-effort mission, more than 130 B-29s took off from seven bomber bases throughout the U.S. The formations converged on their target in a mock bombing raid on New York, Philadelphia, Washington, and other major eastern cities, theoretically dropping their bombs. The photo shows part of the formation that attacked Los Angeles. In front of the picture is B-29A 44-61938 from the 492nd Bombardment Squadron, 7th Bombardment Group, at Fort Worth Air Force Base, Texas. Photo: U.S. Air Force.

Chapter Three - Global capability

A Boeing B-29A from the 19th Bombardment Group touches down at North West Field, Guam. In 1947, it was the only operational B-29 within the U.S. Far East Air Force (USFEAF). In the background, several Superfortresses are visible with the 19th Group's code Black "Square M" on the tail. Photo: U.S. Air Force.

to European bases, on training missions in order not to further alarm worried-European governments. The permanent stationing of the heavy bombers at bases in Europe was out of the question for the time being. In Asia, it was a different story. There was less likelihood of international trouble over the deployments to Japan, where the Americans were virtually the sole occupying power. In November 1947, the 9th Bombardment Squadron of the 7th Bombardment Group prepared for a thirty-day training deployment to Yokota, Japan. On November 6, four B-29s took off from their home base, Fort Worth Army Air Field, Texas, for Naval Air station Barbers Point on O'ahu, Hawaii. At Hawaii, it was discovered that the fuel used in the Pacific was not compatible for the B-29s. Based on that, the B-29s were recalled to Forth Worth.[38] It took six months for the fuel plants at the Japanese air bases to be made suitable for the American B-29s that required a much higher octane than the Japanese were used to for their planes.

In May 1947, the Far East Air Force (FEAF) asked for a squadron on rotation to augment its permanent VHB force. At that time, the six heavy bomber bases in the Mariana Islands were reduced to just three; of those, only North Field remained a very heavy bomber base with the 19th Bombardment Group as resident. Harmon Field on Guam continued its logistical and maintenance mission, while Northwest Field, Guam, was a fighter base and home of the 23rd Fighter Group that was equipped with the long-range Republic P-47N Thunderbolt. The Far East B-29 rotations were approved the same month and flights began soon after. As part of Operation Finback, six squadrons of eight aircraft spent a month each at Yokota.[39]

On these moves, that lasted until October 1948, the B-29 crews received training in transoceanic flying and navigation and practiced dropping some live bombs on small desert islands. In November, the project was abruptly terminated due to a shortage of high-grade fuel on Hawaii, where USAF used its bases for the refueling of the bombers and transports on transoceanic ferry flights. Another benefit of these trips to Japan involved testing the Eighth Air Force's mobility plan. Based on experiences with the operations on the Marianas, the SAC staff at Fort Worth compiled a list of items needed for B-29 operations and designed a storage bin that fitted in the bomb bay of a B-29.

With a few C-54 transports supplementing the bombers, a B-29 unit could transport those bins, spare engines, and mechanics to a field overseas and set up an operation on short notice. A squadron of the 7th Bombardment Group successfully tested these kits on a trip to Japan.[40] The practice was trained numerous times to bases in Europe and Asia afterward and proved quite successful.

Assembly hassle

While transportation no longer posed too many problems, the assembly of the atomic bombs did. An atomic bomb consisted of several essential parts that had to be brought together. For safety reasons, the parts were stored separately in secure environments. Such shelter facilities were lacking at foreign bases at that time. Although if the need arose, it could still be provisionally arranged on British air bases, like RAF Lakenheath and RAF Sculthorpe. Because of the distance to the Asian mainland, the nuclear base on Tinian Island, which was used for the atomic attack on Japan, was no threat to the Soviet Union. Experiments were already underway with a less complex loading method that did not require using a loading pit with a hydraulic elevator. The waiting was for the Boeing B-50, the successor of the B-29, whose nose would be jacked up, allowing the bomb to be rolled under the bomb bay. But that was not yet the case in 1947. On top of that, the Mark I Little Boy (Hiroshima) and Mark III Fat Man (Nagasaki) were essentially laboratory weapons.

Assembling the bombs took a crew of fifty people over twenty-four hours, and once assembled, the bomb had to be dropped within forty-eight hours, or the batteries would die and the entire device would have to be disassembled. The Special Weapons Project (AFSWP), which was formed in early 1947, provided military training in complex nuclear weapons operations. It worked closely with the 38th Engineer Battalion (Special) at Sandia Base, the principal nuclear weapons installation of the United States Department of Defense near Albuquerque, New Mexico. Throughout the year, they worked to simplify the assembly method, training all three Army units to work together in the complex process.

Airborne assembly lab

One such combined training took place in August 1947, at Davis-Monthan Air Force Base in Tucson, Arizona. Under code name Cowboy, five nukes were assembled using modified C-97 aircraft, code-named Chickenpox, to determine if the plane could be used as a forward assembly site. One of the C-97s contained an airborne assembly laboratory built into the aircraft. Other C-97s would carry a portable assembly building. By the time the fifth bomb had been assembled, the teams were completely exhausted.[41] The sixteen hours suggested assembly time proved impossible to meet. However, this Cowboy exercise indicated that the Chickenpox C-97 assembly laboratory could be used operationally.[42]

As part of the project Chickenpox, Boeing XC-97 43-27470 and six YC-97 Stratofreighters (serials 45-59587/92) were converted for the transport, mobile assembly, and maintenance of atomic weapons. All six belonged to the 1st Air Transport Unit (ATU) of the 58th Bombardment Wing, the parent organization of the nuclear 509th Bombardment Group. Initially, the 1st ATU was stationed at Fort Worth, Texas, the headquarters base of SAC's Eighth Air Force. In 1947, the squadron moved to Biggs Air Field, Texas, where the 97th Bombardment Group also moved that year. The 97th came from Smoky Hill Air Field, from where it deployed to Europe several times.
Left: Stratofreighter 45-59589 wears the postwar buzz code "CS" on the fuselage, identifying it as a C-97. Visible in the background is a second Chickenpox C-97. Photo: Boeing.

Chapter Three - Global capability

The assumption of the U.S. Joint War Planning Committee was that the U.S. would possess 100-200 atomic bombs on D-day. The plan called for dropping 34 atomic bombs on 24 cities in Russia, Ukraine, Azerbaijan, and Georgia. Moscow would be hit by seven bombs, Leningrad three, and Karkov and Stalingrad each by two. The rest of the cities would be bombed by one bomb each. It would be carried out by B-29s and B-50s operating from bases in England, Pakistan, and Japan, while intercontinental B-36s would be flown from bases in the continental USA, Alaska, and Greenland. The planners hoped that these attacks would bring enormous physical and psychological damage that might force the Soviet Union to capitulate immediately. The reality, however, would be a Soviet offensive that would overrun Western Europe, parts of the Middle East, and North China. From forward bases, the USAF would begin air offensive against Soviet industry, people, and morale. The planners felt that the Soviet Union might capitulate, in which case the U.S., England, and Canada would send forces into Russia to police the surrender. For this plan, the Air Force and Navy would need more than 90,000 aircraft, a requirement that would call for a massive and unrealistic production effort. It was recognized that Broiler was not adequate as a basis for mobilization planning, and accordingly, a new joint outline plan was developed for war against the Soviet Union during 1955/56. Like the short-range Broiler (1947) - and the Bushwacker (1948), and Halfmoon (1949) war plans - the guidance for the new long-range plan, designated Charioteer, assumed the loss of Western Europe and the need for a massive atomic air campaign launched from bases in the U.S., England, Greenland, Iceland, Alaska, the Middle East, Pakistan, Okinawa, and Japan. Using new bombers like the Boeing B-47 and Convair B-36, the USAF's bombing campaign would be aimed at Russian atomic production centers and storage sites, followed by political and administrative centers and industrial sites.

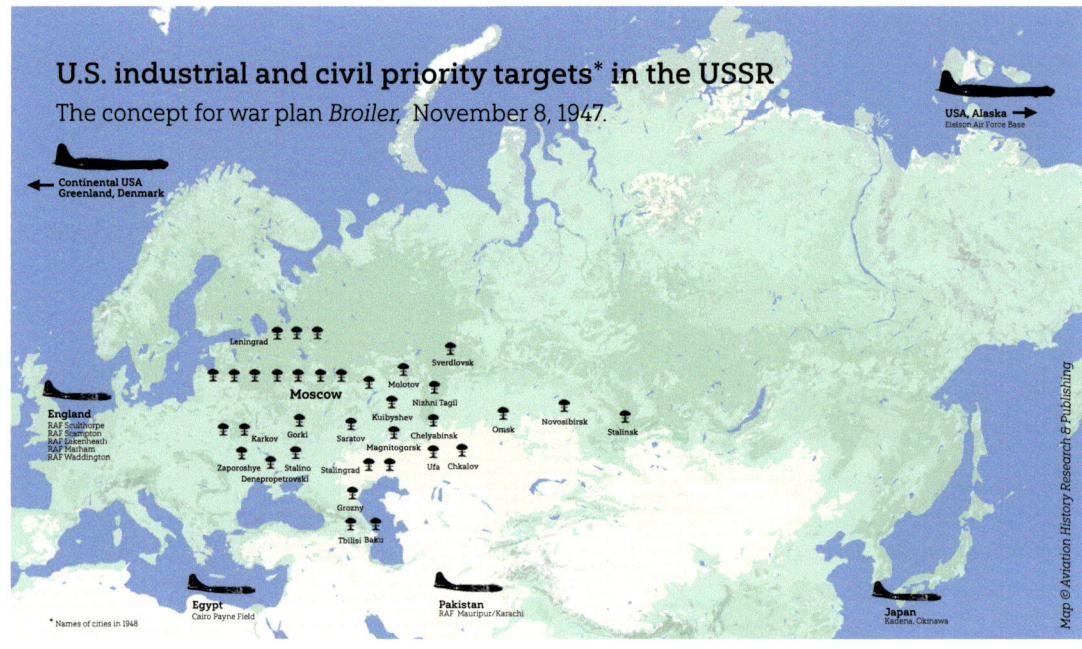

And thus, USAF became—at least in theory—less dependent on the presence of loading and arming facilities at foreign airfields. It is doubtful that the Chickenpox approach has ever been practiced outside the U.S. Indeed, as tensions grew between East and West, so did the willingness of the British government, in particular, to make Britain's RAF airfields suitable for nuclear use worldwide and to station whole groups of American B-29s in their country.

Only two B-29 groups prepared for war

Although SAC by December 31, 1947, had a strength of 44,000, equipped with 319 B-29s in eleven groups and 350 fighters, 230 F-51 Mustangs and 120 F-80 Shooting Stars, only two B-29 groups were fully operational and prepared for war. And only one—the 509th Bombardment Group—of these had atomic capability.[43] The second group in line to transition to the atomic mission was the 43rd Bombardment Group. But there were not enough modified B-29s to even begin with the process.[44] The number of modified B-29s capable of delivering the atomic bomb was far too small to carry out the war plans of SAC as outlined by the Joint War Plans Committee in *Concept of Operations for Pincher*.

At the beginning of 1947, there were 25 operational Silverplate B-29s left of the 49 built. Eighteen were in storage with the Air Material Command at the Aerospace Maintenance and Regeneration Group at Davis-Monthan, Arizona, four were destroyed, and two were in use for the Project W-47 of the Manhattan nuclear energy program at Kirtland Field, Albuquerque, New Mexico.[45]

Within two years, the number of heavy nuclear bombers had to increase to comply with the Pentagon requirement of 225 very heavy atomic bombers by January 1949. The Air Material Command directed the Silverplate (19 additional B-29s) and the post-1947 Saddletree (80 B-29s, 105 B-50s, and 18 B-36s) modernization programs, which, together with the already operational bombers would slightly exceed the target. In 1947, if the international situation were to deteriorate in the near future and with worsening U.S.-Soviet relations, this was not unthinkable; there would be little that SAC could do.[46]

Showing muscles and teeth

SAC could show its muscles and teeth and demonstrate to the Soviets that it could make its mark worldwide. Strategic Air Command demonstrated that with massive mock attacks on key cities in the U.S. It had to show the Russians that the USAF could warn and deploy large numbers of bombers and fighters for long-range attacks. On April 11, 1947, a flight of 64 B-29s from seven squadrons of the three Very Heavy Bombardment Groups (7th, 43rd, and 509th) provided an aerial overview over Fort Worth, Dallas, Carlsbad, El Paso, Tucson, Phoenix, and Riverside. The largest flight of B-29s since World War II headed for a simulated bombing run on Los Angeles.[47] With tension mounting in Europe, Harry Truman knew the situation on the ground was untenable. Unlike the U.S., the Soviet Union kept its army together after the war. It had 15 divisions with more than 350,000 troops in Germany, while the U.S. had only 60,000 occupation troops in Germany. But Moscow did not yet have the bomb. The Soviets still had 180 divisions in Western Russia that they could throw into Germany.

The U.S. had the bomb, three of which had been tested for sheer power in April and May 1948. And the U.S. had a strategic air force, better and technologically superior to its Soviet counterpart. America had the B-29 that had wiped out Hiroshima and Nagasaki, its potent B-50 successor, and the mighty intercontinental B-36 bomber that was coming. More importantly, the U.S. had established a network of well-equipped airfields encircling the Soviet Union. From bases in Spain, Germany, Japan, Alaska, Libya, Egypt, and thanks to many overseas deployments with trained crews, the USAF could hit the USSR wherever and whenever it wanted.

From 1947, SAC received large numbers of F-80 Shooting Star jet fighters. They replaced the outdated F-51 Mustang and F-47 Thunderbolt propeller-driven escort fighters. The second-nearest to the camera is F-80A 44-85364, which went to the 71st Fighter Squadron of the 1st Fighter Group at March Field, California. In 1949, this unit was re-equipped with North American F-86 fighter-interceptors. Photo: Lockheed.

The 7th Bombardment Group was the first SAC unit to receive the Convair B-36 Peacemaker. In June 1948, the first B-36s arrived at Fort Worth Army Air Field (later renamed Carswell Air Force Base), Texas, replacing the units B-29s that were transferred to the 97th Bombardment Group at Biggs Air Force Base, El Paso, Texas. The enormous six-engined Convair bomber was the largest aircraft ever to serve with the USAF. It had atomic bomb-carrying capacity and an intercontinental range. On 7 December, a B-36B similar to 44-92033 (left) demonstrated its enormous reach by flying a nonstop simulated bombing mission to Hawaii, dropping a 10,000 lb simulated bombload in the ocean. The flight took over thirty-five hours and covered over 8,000 miles (12,875 kilometers). Photo: U.S. Air Force.

Chapter Four

Soviet conduct

A line of nine Tupolev Tu-4 Bull bombers of the Russian Air Force (VVS). In essence, the Tu-4 was the spitting image of the B-29, perfectly and in detail copied by the Russians, except for the engines, the electronics, and the fire control. For reverse engineering, the Tupolev design bureau used four B-29s - three B-29s that made emergency landings in Soviet territory during World War II and one that crashed in Russia. The Tu-4 entered service in 1948 and was capable of delivering atomic bombs. The Tu-4 possessed sufficient range to attack Chicago or Los Angeles from bases in the Soviet Union on a one-way mission. Photo: VVS.

The Soviet Union lacked a strategic air force for an offensive against the U.S. What remained for the Soviets was the threat of a land war in Europe; the overrun of Germany, the Netherlands, Belgium, and Denmark from Copenhagen to Palermo and Gibraltar, and Greece, Turkey, and Iran would not escape either. American hopes were that the nuclear threat would cause the Soviets to repent and cease their Communist imperialism and subjugation of countries in Eastern Europe and Asia.

According to the U.S. Joint Strategic Planning Group (JSPG), the Soviet Union's ultimate goal was Soviet domination of a Communist world. Moscow's immediate aim was to establish a barrier—an iron curtain—of Soviet-dominated states around Russia's borders. In 1947, the U.S. did not believe that the Soviet Union was seeking an armed conflict with the West soon. Instead, they sought to expand their communist influence by means short of a war.[48]

It was George F. Kennan, a Foreign Service Officer with long experience in the Soviet Union and Director of the State Department's elite Policy Planning Staff, whose 1947 article in Foreign Affairs, entitled *The Sources of Soviet Conduct*, introduced the term "containment." The policy of firm containment was designed to confront the Russians with unalterable counterforce at every point where they showed signs of encroaching upon the interests of a peaceful and stable world. Kennan believed that if the United States exerted sufficient economic, political, and diplomatic pressure, it would significantly improve Soviet behavior. Though Kennan acknowledged that military forces were a vital diplomatic tool, he doubted whether the United States and the Soviet Union would ever go to war.[49]

The military planners in the Pentagon thought differently. They believed a war between the U.S. and the Soviet Union was just a matter of time. In July 1947, the Joint War Plans Committee concluded that the tension between East and West had progressed far enough to justify the preparation of a joint war plan for the initial stages of a war beginning within the next three years. The Joint War Plans Committee directed the Joint Strategic Planning Group to prepare the joint war plan Broiler for hostilities forced upon the United States by Soviet aggression. It was assumed that atomic weapons would be used by the United States.[50] The Planning Group assumed a war with the Soviet Union during fiscal 1948 (July 1947 – June 1948) and that the implementation would require the mobilization of the U.S. forces to be completed by March 1948. Although a massive atomic attack would require far fewer ground troops than a conventional attack, that date could still be met—assuming SAC had its fleet of strategic bombers in order and a sufficient stockpile of atomic bombs. Both were doubtful. Therefore, the war forecast was moved up to the fiscal year 1949. And that meant that the world could expect a U.S. nuclear D-day attack by mid-1950. The U.S. war planners had calculated that they could bomb Moscow to Stone Age with seven Mk.III bombs of twenty-three kilotons each.

Breaking the nuclear monopoly

Would the Kremlin have known of this planning in Washington? And would they have been aware of the low U.S. nuclear stockpile and marginal nuclear B-29 fleet? Fact of the matter is that Stalin's remarks to Molotov during the Potsdam conference in 1945 had their effect: Russia was well underway with its own nuclear bomb. The production of uranium ore in the Erzgebirge, in the southeastern provinces of Thüringen and Sachsen at the border with the Czech Republic and in the Russian occupied zone of

Germany was in high gear and reached 321 tons in 1948. In the KB-11 nuclear design bureau in the secret town of Sarov, known as Arzamas-16 or "The Installation," Russian scientists and their interned German colleagues were intensively working on the RDS-1, the first Russian atomic bomb. It was just a matter of time and Stalin would have broken the American nuclear monopoly. Why would he worry at all? One thing, however, was itchy to Stalin: the Truman Doctrine.

Truman's Doctrine

On March 12, 1947, in an address before the American Congress, President Harry Truman sketched a portrait of a world divided in two: a democratic free half and a half that was not free but which lived under a Communist regime. He stressed that every country in the world must choose between the two systems but that too often, it would not be a free choice. The crux of his argument was American aid for countries threatened by communism. It was a direct answer to the Marxist-Leninist ideology, the basis of the Communist "world revolution" so feared by the Americans. And not only by them. Truman said: "U.S. foreign policy must be directed

President Harry Truman during an Air Force display on February 15, 1949, at Andrews Air Base, Maryland. He is aboard Convair B-36A, serial number 44-92010, the seventh production bomber, delivered to the USAF in June 1948. Together with General Dwight D. Eisenhower - the temporary chairman of the Joint Chief of Staff - he showed members of his Cabinet the latest developments in aircraft technology. The Boeing B-47 jet bomber, the Northrop XB-49 flying wing bomber, and the North American F-86 Sabre jet fighter were on display and flying. Photo: U.S. Air Force.

Chapter Four - Soviet Conduct

towards supporting free countries who resist attempts of subjugation by armed minorities or through external pressure." This was what commentators called the Truman Doctrine. Later, Truman wrote that this was the turning point in American foreign policy and marked the beginning of American resistance to Communist expansion in Europe and the Middle East. The first countries to profit from American aid were Greece and Turkey. Greece received $250 million ($3,300 million 2023 dollars) in military support and Turkey $150 million ($2,004 million in 2023 dollars). Civilian and military advisors were sent to Greece to assist in the guerrilla war against a Communist takeover. This war had become more tenacious since British troops had left Greece and the Greek Democratic Army (DSE) that was completely controlled by the Greek Communist Party (KKE) was receiving support from neighboring communist countries, particularly from Bulgaria.

As early as July 1947, the Greek air force, the Elliniki Aeroporia, received large numbers of North American AT-6 Texans which were flown to Greece by USAFE pilots. The AT-6 was actually an advanced trainer and was useful as liaison, observation, and light-strike aircraft. The Greek Texans were used against the communist guerrillas with reasonable success. The Greek Air Force were also given Douglas C-47s for troop transport and the rest of the dollar aid went on armoured vehicles, weapons, munitions, and improvements to the military infrastructure, such as radar.

Within the framework of the Truman Doctrine, the U.S. sent military advisors to supervise the modernization of the Turkish military forces. For financial reasons, the British government was forced to leave the modernization of the Turkish military force to the United States, As early as August 1946, the U.S. had sharply criticized the Soviets' claim to the Dardanelles. When part of the U.S. fleet steamed towards the eastern Mediterranean—in the midst of the Yugoslav crisis following the shooting down of an American C-47 transport plane in Slovenia—General Dwight D. Eisenhower declared without any compromise that the Soviet Union would not take a step that would irrevocably lead to a war.[51] With this, he made it clear to the Russians that the Americans were not afraid of a hard confrontation over the Dardanelles. The U.S. also established several support posts that were used by the U.S. Army and USAFE for exercises. Several Turkish airfields were proposed for permanent use by USAF units. This use would not be for peaceable purpose only because Turkey, thanks to its unique strategic location on the Black Sea and bordering on the Soviet Republics of Armenia and Georgia, could count on a lot of interest from the American information services.

"Blatant American imperialism"

After World War II, most of the European infrastructure lay in ruins. Harbors, railways, bridges, utilities, industry, and whole cities, all lay in rubble—with millions of refugees and massive stagnation in agriculture and industrial output. The Soviet Union controlled most of Eastern Europe, and this expansionism made Western European countries vulnerable to a heightened sense of crisis.

In a speech at Harvard University on June 5, 1947, U.S. Secretary of State George Marshall

*During the Greek Civil War, the Royal Hellenic Air Force employed three squadrons of British- and American-surplus North American T-6D and T-6G Harvards/Texans for close air support, observation, and artillery spotting duties. From July 1947 to May 1948, USAFE pilots ferried the Texans to Greece as a part of U.S. assistance in suppressing the Communist guerrilla revolt. USAFE also transferred three C-47s. This military assistance to Greece (and Turkey) implemented the Truman Doctrine, which President Truman had proclaimed in response to the growing communist threat in the world.
Photo: U.S. Air Force.*

proposed that European nations create a plan for their economic reconstruction and that the United States provide financial support and economic assistance. Marshall was convinced that Europe's economic woes threatened Europe's political stability more than the Soviet Union. What was needed to prevent future war was military strength and economic well-being.[52] On July 12, 1947, delegations from sixteen European nations convened in Paris. They represented Austria, Belgium, Denmark, France, Greece, Iceland, Ireland, Italy, Luxembourg, the Netherlands, Norway, Portugal, Sweden, Switzerland, Turkey, and the United Kingdom. It had been hoped that Czechoslovakia and Poland, at least, would participate in the Eastern bloc; indeed, the Czechs initially agreed to attend the conference as observers. However, Moscow forced them and the other Eastern European countries to follow the party line, denouncing the Marshall Plan as blatant American imperialism.[53]

To the dismay of the Soviets, President Truman confirmed Marshall's ideas in a message to Congress on December 19, 1947. Soon, Truman would sign the Economic Recovery Act outlining the U.S. assistance to restore the economic infrastructure of postwar Europe. The four-year recovery plan—known as the Marshall Plan—was worth $13.3 billion (about $169 billion in 2023 dollars) to rebuild the European economy, provide markets for U.S. goods, and support the development of stable democracies in Western Europe.

A North Atlantic pact

When President Truman informed the U.S. Congress of the recovery plan, Secretary of State Marshall met with his British colleague, foreign secretary Ernest Bevin, in London and discussed the formation of the Western European Union. This union was the European military alliance established between France, the United Kingdom, and the three Benelux countries, Belgium, Netherlands, and Luxembourg. If the Western European countries were to engage in defense cooperation, as envisioned in the Marshall Plan, they could count on U.S. support, Marshall maintained to Bevin. The die was cast from a North Atlantic military pact on a path of global bipolar confrontation; this was how the Russians perceived it. Stalin became alarmed by the launch of the Marshall Plan and the establishment of a Western Union (WU), which in his eyes, made the heartlands of Western Europe more resistant to Soviet power and influence.

The Soviets kept their divisions behind the Iron Curtain at war strength. They increased the pressure through communist/socialist movements in Czechoslovakia, Romania, Hungary, and Poland, as well as in countries like Italy, France, and Finland. In doing so, the Russians further aroused American fears of the overthrow of democracies by the Specter of Communism. An overthrow of the government in Italy and elsewhere by Communists instilled such fear in the Americans that they pulled out all the diplomatic and military stops and sent the CIA out with all sorts of obscure activities to prevent Communist takeovers in Europe.[54]

American fighters and bombers over Berlin

The developments harmed the more or less friendly relationship between the Allies in Berlin. Social meetings gradually decreased;

During 1947 and the build-up of the Berlin Crisis in 1948, small deployments of B-29 squadrons were stationed at Fürstenfeldbruck Air Base. The squadron rotation program ended in July 1948 when the Russian initiation of the Berlin Blockade created a sufficient impetus for the long-sought establishment of a 90-day group rotation program to Europe. The first group at Fürstenfeldbruck was the Fifteen Air Force's 301st Bombardment Group from Smoky Hill Air Force Base, Kansas. While in Europe, the 301st was under the operational control of the United States Air Forces in Europe (USAFE). Their training included familiarization flights and aerial reviews over Western Europe, radar bombing, and navigational training flights.
The photo from May 1948 shows an RB-29 reconnaissance plane during take-off at Fürstenfeldbruck Air Base. According to the official caption of this photo, the RB-29 is from the 16th Photographic Reconnaissance Squadron. Besides regular deployments of standard B-29s for training missions, the USAF also sent small detachments of RB-29s to Europe for spy missions along the borders of the Iron Curtain and in the Berlin air corridors. Photo: U.S. Air Force.

Chapter Four - **Soviet Conduct**

tion, General Clay, the U.S. military governor in Germany, on May 30, had a U.S. fighter group fly over Berlin in an impressive formation making the letters "US." Clay believed it somewhat diverted the trend in the war of nerves.[55]

A week later, he ordered several B-29s to fly over Berlin. It was expected that this action would provoke a sharp protest from the Soviets. It did. Clay replied that because of concerns about Soviet occupation forces being large enough to secure Berlin, he felt it necessary to determine the effectiveness with which the U.S. could participate in security arrangements. Whether such replies were helpful to ease the tension in Germany and Berlin, in particular, is rather doubtful.

The formation of fighter planes most likely was formed by Republic F-47s of the 86th Fighter Group based at Neubiberg since they were, at the time, the only USAFE operational fighter group with sufficient planes and trained pilots to perform the special formation over Berlin. The only B-29s in Europe at the time of the demonstration over Berlin were from the 97th Bombardment Group that was stationed at Giebelstadt Air Base in June 1947.

Coup in Prague

Russia began a public relations offensive through the German media channels they controlled and, with indoctrination, incited the

In June 1948, USAFE consisted of one tactical fighter group, two troop carrier groups, and a photoreconnaissance squadron, while reinforcements in one fighter group were expected in a few months. The 86th Fighter Group at Neubiberg Air Base consisted of three squadrons with seventy-five WWII-vintage Republic F-47 Thunderbolts. The group was well-trained, had experienced officers, and boasted a 90 percent operational efficiency rating. The 45th Reconnaissance Squadron at Fürstenfeldbruck Air Base was a composite unit of twenty-one Douglas A-26 and FA-26s, North American F-6s (reconnaissance version of the P-51 Mustang), and Boeing B-17s. This unit, too, was experienced and well-trained with an 85 percent operational efficiency rating. Additionally, as part of the Strategic Air Command's rotational training, one squadron of Boeing B-29 Superfortresses was in residence at Fürstenfeldbruck in Bavaria. USAF photos above and to the right: F-47D's 44-89817 and 44-89869, both from the 527th FS, 86th FG, Neubiberg, Munich. Photo's: U.S. Air Force/via Merle Olmsted.

it soon became apparent that fewer Russians were attending the Allied social functions and informal meetings between senior representatives came to a standstill. It is a common Soviet way of indicating displeasure. In the early months of 1947, the Soviet-controlled German press in Berlin started publishing rumors of the Soviet army and air force strength in Germany. Soon after, the Soviets had their fighter planes demonstratively flown over Berlin. In a reac-

workers' parties in Italy and France against US economic and military plans and provoked the disruption of public order with organized demonstrations and strikes. They failed in their scheme to use Italy and France to thwart the creation of a Western economic and military alliance. But Russia did strengthen its sphere of influence in the countries where it had expelled the Nazis. That initially applied to Czechoslovakia, the only country in their sphere of influence that bordered directly on Germany and the American-controlled Allied zone.

In Czechoslovakia, a democratic coalition governed in which non-Communists held the majority. The Soviet Union had significant influence over the country, which was anti-Western mainly because the West had abandoned it before World War II and Adolf Hitler was able to annex the Czech Sudetenland with the Munich Treaty (1938) in his back pocket. The British and French thought it would prevent a war with Germany; the Nazis deceived them and the rest of the world. In 1947, the country was hit by food shortages and accepted American food aid to deal with the problem. Jan Masaryk, the Czech foreign minister, also applied to participate in the Marshall Plan, but Moscow put a stop to that. Russian foreign minister Molotow worked on a Russian economic recovery plan for the Soviet Union and told Masaryk what Czechoslovakia had to do.

"I went to Moscow as foreign minister of an independent sovereign state and came back as a lackey of the Soviet government," Masaryk confided to British Ambassador to Prague Philip Nichols.[56] Moscow tightened the reins and took maximum advantage of a crisis in the Prague government that had arisen partly in response to failed attacks by the Communist militia of several non-Communist ministers. Twelve conservative ministers had resigned over the controversy over the abrupt dismissal of eight non-Communist police chiefs. They were simply replaced by Communists ministers in a violent coup that involved strikes and demonstrations by armed militias.

On February 24, 1948, the coup was completed, causing a shock in the West. The methods used did not differ greatly from those which had already been applied in the Balkans and elsewhere; this was, however, the first forcible Communist conquest of a strongly based free government. In the eyes of most Western people, it put an altogether new light upon the power, ferocity, and scope of Communist aggression.[57] This was heightened after the mysterious death of the 61-year-old Jan Masaryk. On March 10, 1948, he was found dead in the garden of the office of the Foreign Ministry in Prague.

Suicide, the Communists knew. Murder, said the conservative opponents. And they were proven right fifty-nine years and countless investigations later; in 2004, after a rehashed police investigation, it finally was confirmed that he had been pushed out the window by militant Communists. Stalin's long arm reached far beyond the Kremlin; so much was clear.

Washington in shock

In the Pentagon, the shock over Jan Masaryk's death was great. American newspapers were full of rumors and omens of a coming war. President Truman addressed both houses of Congress seven days after the Prague coup and condemned the Soviets, whom he accused of engaging in brutal power politics to subjugate all of Europe. James V. Forrestal, sworn in as the country's first Secretary of Defense on September 17, 1947, wrote in his diaries about the change that all of Europe lies flat while the Russian mafia waltzes over it. "We will then face a war under difficult conditions and with a good chance of losing it," he speculated. Forrestal believed it was inconceivable that even the gang that ruled Russia in 1948 would be willing to go to war. But he remembered that in 1939, Hitler had no reason to start a war, yet he started it with a practically unprepared world. He wanted the Russians to understand that it was folly to continue their aggression. It would lead to war, or if it was impossible to bring them back to their senses, the U.S. would at

Lieutenant General Curtis LeMay (1906-1990) was photographed circa 1948 as a three-star general. During the war, LeMay was the commander of the 305th Bombardment Group from RAF Grafton Underwood during the bombing campaign against Germany. On Jan. 27, 1943, the group participated in the Eighth Air Force's first raid on Germany. LeMay pioneered many daylight bombing techniques used by the USAAF over Nazi-controlled Europe. In the fall of 1944, LeMay was transferred to the war in the Far East. He commanded subsequent B-29 Superfortress combat operations against Japan, including massive incendiary attacks on 67 Japanese cities and the atomic bombings of Hiroshima and Nagasaki.
His motto was: "If you kill enough of them, they will stop fighting." He was known for his radical spirit and conservative personality and was openly a supporter of massive nuclear retaliation. He once said, "If you are going to use military force, then you ought to use overwhelming force. Use too much and deliberately use too much; you'll save lives, not only your own, but the enemy's too."
In 1947, he became the commander of the United States Air Forces in Europe, a clear signal the U.S. could not send to the Russians. Photo: U.S. Air Force.

Chapter Four - **Soviet Conduct**

American forces waited on the Elbe River in the war's closing days while the Russians captured Berlin. The Americans joined the Russians in occupying Berlin on July 2, 1945, when the first American troops landed at Tempelhof Central Airport in C-47s flown in from Halle, Germany, by the 301st Troop Carrier Squadron. The photo shows the arrival of high-ranking officials at Tempelhof in 1945. Besides the VIP C-47 in front of the ceremony, two more C-47s are parked on the tarmac in front of the airport building. In the background, a silver-painted B-17G is visible.
Photo: Author's collection.

least have a beginning to avoid being overrun, as in 1941, when Japan attacked Pearl Harbor.[58]

Problems in Berlin

Meanwhile, in Germany, tension was rising over Berlin. The fact that Berlin had not come under complete Soviet control after the war had always been a thorn in Russia's side. At the Potsdam conference in 1945, the three Allies decided that each of them would occupy a sector of the city. Like Vienna, Berlin was roughly divided into a Western Zone of Occupation (America, Britain, and later France) and an Eastern Zone of Occupation (Russia). City administration remained a joint task for which an Allied Control Council was established. The commanders of all four Allies served on the Council. From the first Council meeting, the Russians insisted that each Western Ally be responsible for the facilities in their sector. The Allies also decided that all Council decisions should be unanimous. Problems arose after only a few meetings. The Russians wanted to stick to all the measures they had taken before forming the Allied Control Council. And because the Russians had the right of veto, all their actions remained. Only when it was too late, did the Western Allies realize their grave mistake. They had approved an administration in which the Communists managed or controlled vital functions, such as the movement of money, the police, the trade unions, the political parties, and the press, which distributed exclusively Communist propaganda. All could have gone better in that consultation with the Russians, and it was only a matter of time before this led to significant problems.

Uneasy feeling

It was the uneasy feeling that the Russians had a hidden agenda for Berlin and were after something entirely different. What exactly that was, even General Lucius D. Clay did not know. He was Commander in Chief of the United States Air Forces in Europe and military governor of the United States Zone, deputizing General Dwight D. Eisenhower in 1945. Not a dumb guy, in other words. The Russians' behavior bothered him so deeply that on March 5, he sent an alarming "eyes-only" telegram to Lieutenant General Stephen J. Chamberlin, Director of Intelligence, Army General Staff. "For many months, based on logical analysis, I have believed and judged that war was unlikely for at least a decade," Clay wrote. "In the last few weeks, I have sensed a subtle change in the attitude of the Soviet Union, which I cannot define, but now makes me feel that it could suddenly be dramatic. I cannot support this change in my own thinking with any data or outward evidence other than to describe it as a feeling of a new tense in every Soviet person with whom we have official relations. In the absence of supporting data, I cannot give an official report, but my feeling is real. You may advise the Chief of Staff on this, for what it is worth, if you deem it advisable.[59]

Constant disagreements

At the end of World War II, air raids on Berlin had left the city little more than smoldering rubble. Most of the destruction resulted from the night raids that the RAF Bomber command had systematically carried out during the last months of the war. In April and May 1945, the Russian First Army and the remnants of the German army fought bitter, street-by-street battles in ruins. After the surrender, the eastern part of Berlin came under the harsh Russian regime, and the population cowered under the Communist terror of fanatical and brutal Russian troops. The stream of refugees from the eastern regions seeking safe shelter in Western Berlin grew from thousands during the war's final months to hundreds of thousands in the first postwar months. The city, 120 kilometers deep in Russian-occupied East Germany, was a thorn in the Russians' side. From the beginning, Berlin was the scene of political skirmishes. That began as early as the July 1945 conference of the Allies in Potsdam, where they arranged the division of Europe and where the future borders were determined. Constant disagreements, fueled by the political differences between Western capitalism and Soviet communism, caused irritations in the Allied camp. At Potsdam, it had been agreed that fifteen percent of all equipment dismantled in the Western German zones—especially from the metallurgical, chemical, and machine manufacturing industries from the Ruhr area—would be transferred to the Soviets in return for food, coal, agri fertilizers, timber, petroleum products, etc. Western deliveries started in 1946, as agreed. The Soviet deliveries were desperately needed to provide the millions of eastern expellees with food, heat, and basic necessities and to increase agricultural production in the remaining cultivation area. But the Soviet deliveries did not materialize at all. Consequently, General Lucius D. Clay stopped the transfer of dismantled industries to the Soviet sector in May 1946 while the expellees from the areas under Soviet rule were deported to the West. As a reaction to the halt of deliveries from the Western zones, the Soviet Union began to obstruct the administrative work of all four zones.

Escalating tensions

When in January 1947, the United States and the United Kingdom unified their respective zones and formed the Bizone, Berlin became the epicenter of the escalating tensions between East and West. At the end of February 1948, the United States, United Kingdom, and France secretly began to plan the creation of a new German federal state made up of the Western Allies' occupation zones. In March, when the Soviets discovered these intentions, the situation reached a boiling point. The main goal of the Soviet leadership was to persuade the USA, the United Kingdom, and France to suspend preparations for creating the Western German state. On March 19, 1948, Stalin met with German leaders of the Soviet-controlled Party of Socialist German Unity (SED). The German Communist leader Wilhelm Pieck complained that the presence of the Americans, British, and French in Berlin threatened to disrupt elections scheduled for 1949. "Let's make a joint effort then," Stalin told him, "and perhaps we can kick them out." The following day the Soviets made a fuss during a meeting of the Allied Control Council, which had met regularly since the war's end to coordinate occupation policy between zones.

In an attempt to pressure the Western leaders to reverse course, Stalin began restricting rail and road traffic between Western Germany and Berlin on April 1. In a swift reaction, General Lucius Clay and Major General Curtis E. LeMay, commander of United States Air Force, decided to airlift supplies to the military garrisons of Berlin using Douglas C-47 transports.

Later dubbed The Little Lift, this operation quickly began delivering as much as eighty tons of U.S. Army rations and perishables like fresh milk, eggs, and vegetables daily.[60] On the instruction of LeMay, USAFE officers quickly established an airlift system. Rhein-Main served as the traffic control point, setting shipment priorities based on Berlin requisitions. While flight and maintenance crews did help loading and unloading the C-47s, German civilians did most of the heavy labor at both ends of the operation. There were still enough U.S. C-47 cargo planes available in Germany to carry out the daily delivery of supplies to the garrisons in Berlin. Still, the primary problem was the shortage of

In 1945, General Lucius DuBignon Clay (1897 - 1978) was assigned by President Franklin D. Roosevelt as deputy military governor in Germany under General Dwight D. Eisenhower. Two years later, he was elevated to commander-in-chief of the U.S. forces in Europe and military governor of the U.S. Zone in Germany. During the war, he primarily served stateside in several administrative positions centered on engineering and logistics. He was a super official with a profound understanding of the organization. His nicknames were: "The Great Uncompromiser" and "The Kaiser." Photo: U.S. Army.

aircrews. Overtaxed airmen ate on the run and napped in odd corners when they could find the time. USAFE operations were shifted away from Tempelhof in Berlin to the less vulnerable located Rhein-Main near Frankfurt. The 53rd Troop Carrier Squadron moved permanently from Tempelhof to Rhein-Main, where it was originally based until the summer of 1947.[61] All but essential maintenance at Tempelhof was transferred to West German bases like the USAFE Air Depots at Oberpfaffenhofen and Erding near München. On April 5, the crisis intensified when a Soviet Yak-3 fighter near Gatow Airport in the British zone of Berlin buzzed a British Viking airliner carrying ten passengers. On the second pass, the Yak hit the Viking head-on taking it down. There were no survivors.[62] On April 10, the Soviet Union relaxed the land route restrictions, and the crisis eased. But the airlift continued, in case Stalin would change his mind.

In the meantime, the Russians were quite annoyed with the air corridors that gave the Allies free access to Berlin. During the negotiations between the Allies in 1945, first in Yalta and then in Potsdam, it was so stipulated; the Soviet Union controlled the road, rail, and water connections between the Western sectors and Berlin. And the Western Allies had gained the right to freely use three corridors connecting the Western sectors with Berlin, although there were restrictions. The three corridors ended at the Berlin Control Zone. That was a circle with a radius of twenty miles (thirty-two kilometers) with the Allied Control Council building on Elssholzstrasse in Berlin-Schöneberg at its center. For the use of the air corridors, the members of the Control Council had set rules; for example, each corridor had a width of a mere twenty miles, and it was not permitted to fly higher than 10,000 feet (3,300 meters). Enforcement of these rules was in the hands of the Air Safety Center, which was housed in the same building as the Control Council. The four powers Soviet Union, USA, UK, and France had no further arrangements made for access to Berlin over land and water between them. That lack enabled the Soviets to impose all sorts of bureaucratic controls and, when it suited them, to frustrate connections with all kinds of restrictions. But they couldn't do much against Allied air traffic in the corridors. That must have irritated them immensely. They pulled out all sorts of stops to disrupt air traffic. They did this by holding military exercises in the corridor. Initially, fighter planes flew at high speed through the corridors—the so-called "buzzing"—then the Soviets disrupted the air traffic with large formations of airplanes taking off from air bases in the corridors and at night with searchlights or—more seriously—using live anti-aircraft artillery. And just as the U.S. Air Force tried to intimidate Moscow by conducting mock attacks on its major cities with formations of B-29 bombers, the Russian Air Force did the same by attacking towns in the corridors en masse. Still, they announced such maneuvers, but not so the buzzing by individual fighters with all the dangers that entailed.

"Let them stew in their own juice"

Soviet frustrations ran so high that the Russian representative at the Air Safety Center breezily informed his Western colleagues that allied night flying across the Soviet zone was no longer acceptable. The Soviets accused the Western Allies of breaking safety rules; they even wanted all civilian air traffic diverted from Gatow and Tempelhof to Schönefeld and Johannisthal/Aldershof in the Soviet sector.[63] The Russians took it to the extreme by demanding all Allied military traffic to Staaken, also in the Soviet sector. Clay's answer to all this was simple: ignore and let the Soviets with their demands stew in their own juice.

*The picture is of Douglas C-47A Skytrain 42-92841. Assigned to various troop carrier units after the war, this C-47 became part of the Berlin Airlift in August 1948 when it was assigned to the 60th Troop Carrier Group at Wiesbaden Air Base. In June 1948, the European Air Transport Command (EATC) of USAFE had about one hundred C-47s and a handful of the more modern Douglas C-54 Skymasters in two Troop Transport Groups; the 60th and the 61st.
Photo: U.S. Air Force.*

Chapter Five

Operation Vittles

On June 18, 1948, the United States, Britain, and France, announced plans to create a unified German currency within the next two days. The new currency—the Deutschmark—would apply to their three occupation zones in Western Germany. The purpose of the currency reform was to wrest economic control of the city from the Soviets, enable the introduction of Marshall Plan aid, and curb the black market in the country. According to Stalin, this contradicted the Yalta Conference of February 1945, when it was agreed that the Allies would jointly decide on the future of Germany. The next day, June 19, Marshal Vassily D. Sokolovsky, Soviet Military Governor of eastern Berlin and Clay's counterpart, declared that all of Berlin, including the Western zones, was part of the Soviet zone of eastern Germany. The Soviets announced on June 23, 1948 that its eastern zone of Germany would have its own currency—the Ostmark—and that would also apply to all of Berlin government. The Western powers declared that this eastern currency was not valid in the Western sectors of Berlin. A day later the D-Mark was also introduced in West Berlin. The new currency was flown in the same day by a C-47 Skytrain from Wiesbaden.[64] The British, too, had been shipping in the new Deutsche Marks. Douglas Dakotas of RAF No. 77 Squadron from RAF Broadwell, Oxfordshire, on June 19 and 20, made a series of trips between RAF Uetersen near Hamburg and RAF Gatow in Berlin.[65] The

Douglas C-54D Skymaster 43-17223 on the tarmac of Tempelhof Air Base in Berlin during the airlift in 1948. Before its deployment to Germany to take part in Operation Vittles, this C-54 was assigned to the 20th Troop Carrier Squadron/314th Troop Carrier Group, which was stationed at Albrook Field, Panama. The C-54 served with a number of units in the 1950s. In 1958, it was at Wiesbaden Air Base, where the 7405th Support Squadron used the aircraft for ELINT missions along the Iron Curtain.
Photo: U.S. Air Force.

Aviation History Research & Publishing

Chapter Five - Operation Vittles

Until 1948, the virtually worthless Reichsmark (RM) was the common currency in both the Western zones and the Soviet zone of Germany. In June 1948, the Western Allies introduced the Deutsche Mark (DM) because there was no way to cooperate with the Soviets. The new currency was needed to end the black market. The Soviets took the introduction of the Western Mark as an excuse to block the access roads to West Berlin and, at the same time, to introduce their own Mark in the Soviet occupation zone: the East German Mark. It was the currency reform that created the two Germanies. The new Deutsche Mark was issued on the morning of June 20, 1948, starting at 08:00 hours. Every West German received a one-time payment of DM 40. Savings were heavily devalued: for every 100 RM saved, there was only DM 6.50. In Berlin, the DM was introduced on June 24, 1948. The picture below shows the crowded exchange office at Wittenbergplatz in Berlin. Photo: Bundesarchive.

loads the two Western Allies carried into Berlin were Deutsche Marks similar to those that had been issued in the Western zones but carrying the overprint "B" for Berlin. The angered Soviets on June 24 blocked all major road, rail, and canal links to West Berlin and cut off all electricity supplied to the Western sectors of Berlin by generators in the Soviet sector. The following day, Stalin announced that food deliveries from the Soviet zone would no longer be allowed to reach Western Berlin.

With this reprehensible blockade action, Russia played with the lives of some two million civilians in the Western sectors who were utterly dependent on the Western Allies for their food. For the world, this meant an anxious period that left East and West on the brink of rocky confrontation. U.S. nuclear retaliation hung like a sword over the Soviet Union, which seemingly cared very little.

No budging

The Americans were all the more so divided. Whether or not to stay in Berlin had occupied Washington for months. In a teleconference with the Pentagon on April 10, Clay again shared his concerns. He stated that the U.S. should not leave Berlin unless driven out by force. Clay warned that when Berlin fell, Western Germany would follow: "To hold Europe against Communism, we must not budge. Withdraw, our position in Europe is threatened", he explained to his counterparts in the Pentagon.[66] During the Cold War, President Harry Truman and his successors in the White House would speak of the domino theory that suggested a Communist government in one nation would quickly lead to Communist takeovers in neighboring states, each falling like a row of dominos. When the Russians announced the Berlin blockade on June 24, 1948, and the flow of food from West Germany almost came to a standstill, the world balanced on the brink of a world conflict.

The U.S. military governor in West Germany, General Lucius D. Clay, played a significant role in defining the position of the United States in postwar Europe, determining the shape of West German democracy, and drawing a line against Soviet expansionism. That line began in Berlin.

Clay was a courteous Southerner from a distinguished family; he was a brilliant military administrator known for his refined manners, sharp wit, and formidable will, which his opponents perceived as uncompromising and pushy. General Clay reacted sharply to the blockade and criticized Moscow's attempt to create mass famine, which would be a brutal political lever in modern history. During the build-up of the crisis in the spring of 1948, General Clay and his staff developed a plan to break the blockade. The idea was to send a unit of combat engineers up the autobahn to fix the bridge over the Elbe River at Hohenwarte—a bridge that the Soviets had closed claiming it needed repairs. Clay knew from intelligence reports that the Soviets were bluffing and believed that immediately forcing a blockade was the correct response. But an armed convoy was also a calculated risk, and Clay knew that gaining Washington's approval for such action would be difficult, perhaps impossible. The British, too, had quite a bit of trouble with Clay's tough stance and were appalled by his plans. "If you do that, it'll be war—it's as simple as that," said General Sir Brian Robertson, the British military command-

er in Germany to Clay when he proposed forcing the blockade.[67] On the other hand, British Foreign Secretary Ernest Bevin told the Americans that the Western powers should stand firm in Berlin. Abandoning the city would have serious, if not disastrous, consequences in West Germany and Western Europe. Instead, Bevin, like Clay, wanted all available transport aircraft to be assigned to an airlift. At the same time, Bevin recommended that the U.S. Government deploy additional heavy bombers to Europe.

General Clay agreed to the proposed air reinforcements. After all, he was an advocate of forceful action. According to Clay, the Soviets feared U.S. air power. So, he advised his colleagues in the Pentagon that the arrival of fighter aircraft would be a decisive factor in maintaining Allied resolve. Clay recommended expanding the B-29 force in Germany from one squadron to a whole group of three squadrons, sending additional B-29s to England and possibly to France, and immediately carrying out the movement of a fighter group into Germany planned for August. War planners in Washington knew what they had to do and quickly decided to put the deployments to Europe in motion.

Three options and one solution

The Western powers had just a few options to react to the Soviet's aggressive actions. First, they could yield to Stalin and stop the currency reform that had begun. This option would have ended the development of an independent, democratic West Germany. A second possibility could be to abandon West Berlin, which would give the Soviets their way to absorb West Berlin and its 2.5 million inhabitants into their plans for a Communist East Germany. The third possibility—suggested by Clay—was to force an armored column across eastern Germany to Western Berlin. The expectation of such an action would be another world war, with the significant risk of a Western loss because of the enormous Soviet forces still in Europe even after World War II. None of these options were

realistic. That left the fourth option, actually the solution: the expansion of the airlift that had begun in April to supply the Western garrisons in Berlin by air. A well-organized and extensive airlift was considered capable of providing adequate supplies for the garrisons and the entire civilian population in West Berlin.[68]

As the situation worsened in June, movement by air of supply for the United States military was again initiated on June 19[69], and the plans based upon the experience of the eleven-day April airlift were placed in effect using the 60th and 61st Troop Carrier Groups based then at Kaufbeuren and Rhein-Main. Rhein-Main became the U.S. Army's European Command (EUCOM). In one week, an average of thirty-eight flights were made each day, transporting approximately 130 tons of supplies.

Every available transport aircraft

On June 24, 1948, in response to the blockade, Clay directed his air commander, Major general Curtis LeMay, to have every transport aircraft available to carry supplies to the beleaguered city. Clay asked LeMay to drop all other uses of the U.S. transport aircraft in Europe so that he could place the entire fleet of close to one hundred C-47s (six squadrons in two groups) on the Berlin run. At the same time, logistic arrangements were made for the movement of

*The months of July and August saw Operation Vittles hit by bad weather. Under harsh conditions, the planes had to land at Tempelhof. On the tarmac, food and bags of coal were transferred into ready trucks. In the photo, a CMG 2½-ton 6×6 cargo truck parks in front of the cargo door of C-47A 42-92467. This Skytrain had participated in the Normandy landings four years earlier. It belonged to the 441st Troop Carrier Group and transported paratroopers of the 501st Parachute Infantry Regiment to a drop zone near Sainte-Mère-Église, Normandy, France, as part of the famous Albany parachute combat assault mission on the night of June 5/6, 1944.
Photo: U.S. Air Force.*

Chapter Five - **Operation Vittles**

*Tempelhof shortly after the war in 1945: the 4,987 by 120 feet runway made from pierced steel planking (PSP) is visible in the center of the ruined original airport buildings. To the south, the immense circular structur, designed by Hitler's architect Albert Speer, is less damaged. The huge operations building was constructed in the early '30s and is considered one of the most remarkable in the world. It boasts seven stories underground. During the war, the undergound building housed a Messerschmitt aircraft factory, and a well-equipped hospital. Tempelhof was designed to be Berlin's principal civil airport, but the high apartment buildings surrounding it made approaches difficult for modern aircraft. Parallel to the existing runway, a new 5,750 x 140 feet runway was built to handle incoming traffic flow. Instead of cement for concrete, which was unavailable in Berlin, a compact 18-inch layer of brick rubble from bombed buildings was successfully used as a foundation. The construction of a third parallel runway, 6,150 x 140 feet, with the same brick rubble base, put Tempelhof in a much better position to cope with the growing volume of Airlift traffic from the Rhein-Main and Wiesbaden air bases
Photo: U.S. Air Force.*

food to Wiesbaden Air Base near Frankfurt to be airfreighted to Tempelhof. The next day in Washington, President Truman brought up the Berlin situation at a meeting of his Cabinet. U.S. Secretary of War Kenneth C. Royall informed him about the problems developing on General Clay's emergency airlift, tasked to daily bring in a minimum of 4,500 tons of food, clothing, coal, raw materials, and medicines to the 2.5 million people in the Western sectors. Far too little, obviously, because the three Western sectors consumed 12,000 tons daily, which was transported by road, rail, and water. Ferrying so much freight to Berlin every day would be almost impossible. It would take many hundreds of cargo aircraft. The daily target of Clay's emergency airlift was an absolute minimum based on a basic ration of 1,990 calories per Berliner per day.[70] The Cabinet meeting concluded that "determined steps" be taken to remain in Berlin.[71]

One obvious step to stay in Berlin was taken two days later by President Truman when he directed that General Clay's improvised airlift be put on a regular basis and that every aircraft available to the European Command be pressed into service.

And, so it did. After the first supply flights had begun on June 19, a week later, on June 26, the airlift under the code name Operation Vittles officially began following the example of The Little Lift.

British sprang into action

Simultaneously, the British also sprang into action. The British Air Forces of Occupation (BAFO) had several airfields in Germany east of the Rhine River, close to the Russian Zone of Occupation. The most important were Fassberg, Celle, Bückeburg, Wunstorf, Detmold, and Gütersloh. On June 24, one day before Vittles was officially launched, the British made it clear that they would supply their troops and their dependents in Berlin by air in operation called Knicker. It soon became apparent that an operation that provided the Berlin garrison but left the civilian population starving was not sustainable. On June 29, the airlift was extended to include Operation Carter Paterson to meet at least the minimal needs of Berlin's civilians. Carter Paterson was the name of a well-known British haulage firm. It was an unfortunate name for the operation since the Russians pointed out in their propaganda that the firm was known primarily as a removal company. The British, they sneered, were organizing a flit.[72] A few days later, on July 3, the two operations were combined under the code name Plainfare.[73]

RAF Transport Command threw in several squadrons of Dakotas, which were transferred to Germany from their bases in England. And thanks to a new, longer runway at RAF Gatow in Berlin, English Transport Command could also begin using the four-engine AVRO York transport aircraft for airlift. AVRO had developed the rugged York based on the Lancaster bomber. Depending on the version, the York could carry as much as 16,500 lbs (7,484 kilograms) of cargo. The RAF sought all possible means to increase the airlift capacity. For example, a detachment of Short Sunderland flying boats of RAF No. 201 Squadron was even deployed from Finken-

An airlift plan for Austria

After the war, Austria was, just like Germany, divided into four zones of occupation — a Soviet zone in the east; an American zone west of it; a French zone in the Tyrol and Vorarlberg; and a British one in the southern provinces of Styria and Carinthia. The Western Allies had several airfields in their zone in the western part of Austria. In Vienna, this was not the case. All airfields were in the Russian sector. The two airfields operated by the Western powers, Tulln-Langenlebarn and Schwechat, were several miles outside Vienna's city limits and accessible only through Soviet territory.

The Russians gave the Western Allies the right of passage to and from Vienna. Also, air corridors were designated and formally adopted by the Allied. It was estimated that the Soviets could easily close down both the road and rail links to the Western zones for quite some time, as well as the corridors to the Tulln and Schwechat airfields, claiming "technical difficulties" or "civil disturbances" as pretexts for denying passage to US and other supplies. To reach Vienna by air, at least with small liaison planes — the Western Allies built two small airstrips in the western sectors of Vienna: an American one on the Danube Channel and a British one in front of Schloss Schönbrunn. But both of these airstrips were capable of handling only light aircraft. The construction of an emergency airstrip within the U.S. Zone of Vienna - to serve the U.S. garrison by air - formed part of the detailed Protective Security Plan developed earlier for major emergencies by Lt. Gen. Geoffrey Keyes, the commanding general of U.S. Forces in Austria.

The plan was to build a large airport in Kaiser Ebersdorf, which was in the eleventh district in the British sector. Keyes and Lt. Gen. Curtis LeMay of the U.S. Air Force reached an agreement that the site was considered satisfactory for constructing an airfield in case of an emergency. General Keyes received the orders to stockpile 1.5 million square feet of pierced steel planking (PSP) for two 5,000-feet runways that could handle large numbers of both the C-47 and the larger, four-engine C-54 aircraft. Both airfields were to be completed in just ten weeks. In early September, the feasibility of an airlift operation in Vienna remained in doubt, especially if simultaneous with a new Berlin airlift.

In January 1950, the Joint Strategic Survey Committee reported that a Soviet blockade of Berlin and Vienna would create a most challenging situation perilously close to war. Furthermore, a commitment simultaneously to attempt airlift operations for both Berlin and Vienna would virtually cripple its combat capability in the event of an emergency. In the event of a blockade of both cities, it was estimated Vienna could fall back on the supplies built while the landlines were still open.

As a first measure, an 84-day reserve supply of food was established in Vienna, and a six-month supply of coal. Supplies under the codename Operation Squirrel Cage were stored in up to twenty-eight warehouses dispersed over the Western sectors of the city. The value of the food stocks was estimated at over $17 million in 1948 (210 million in today's money). A blockade of Vienna never materialized. The plans for a relief airlift operation were finally relegated to the archives when Austria regained its independence in 1955.

The stocks were reduced to a 45-day level by January 1954 and a 15-day supply by June 1954. By early 1955, only 1,800 tons of canned horsemeat were left. These were finally sold as dog food—an ignominious end to a once glorious plan to sustain Vienna in the face of Soviet aggression.

Tulln Air Base, now Fliegerhorst Brumowski, was located deep in the Russian Occupation Zone, approximately twenty-one miles west-northwest of Vienna and just south of the Danube River, next to the village of Langenlebarn. The air base was large enough to host transport planes like the Lockheed C-69 Constellation from the U.S. Military Air Transport Service (MATS). PanAm Airways also operated these intercontinental aircraft; from June 1946 to June 1955, PanAm Constellations were regular visitors to Langenlebarn. The photo shows VC-121E "Columbine III" 53-7885, the Presidential aircraft that visited Tulln on May 13, 1955, bringing the U.S. Secretary of State John Foster Dulles to a meeting in Vienna. Photo via Dr. Hubert Prigl/Ruud Leeuw.

Abstract from "The Airlift That Never Was: Allied Plans To Supply Vienna by Air, 1948-1950," (1996) by Dr. Erwin A. Schmidl.

Chapter Five - **Operation Vittles**

Before the 1948 airlift, there were three airfields operating within the Berlin city limits. These were Gatow (constructed in 1934), Tempelhof (1938) as well as Johannisthal/Adlershof (1909). Tegel was put into operation in 1948. Each occupying power had its own airport in its assigned sector. Close to Berlin were four more former Luftwaffe airfields used by the Russian Air Force.

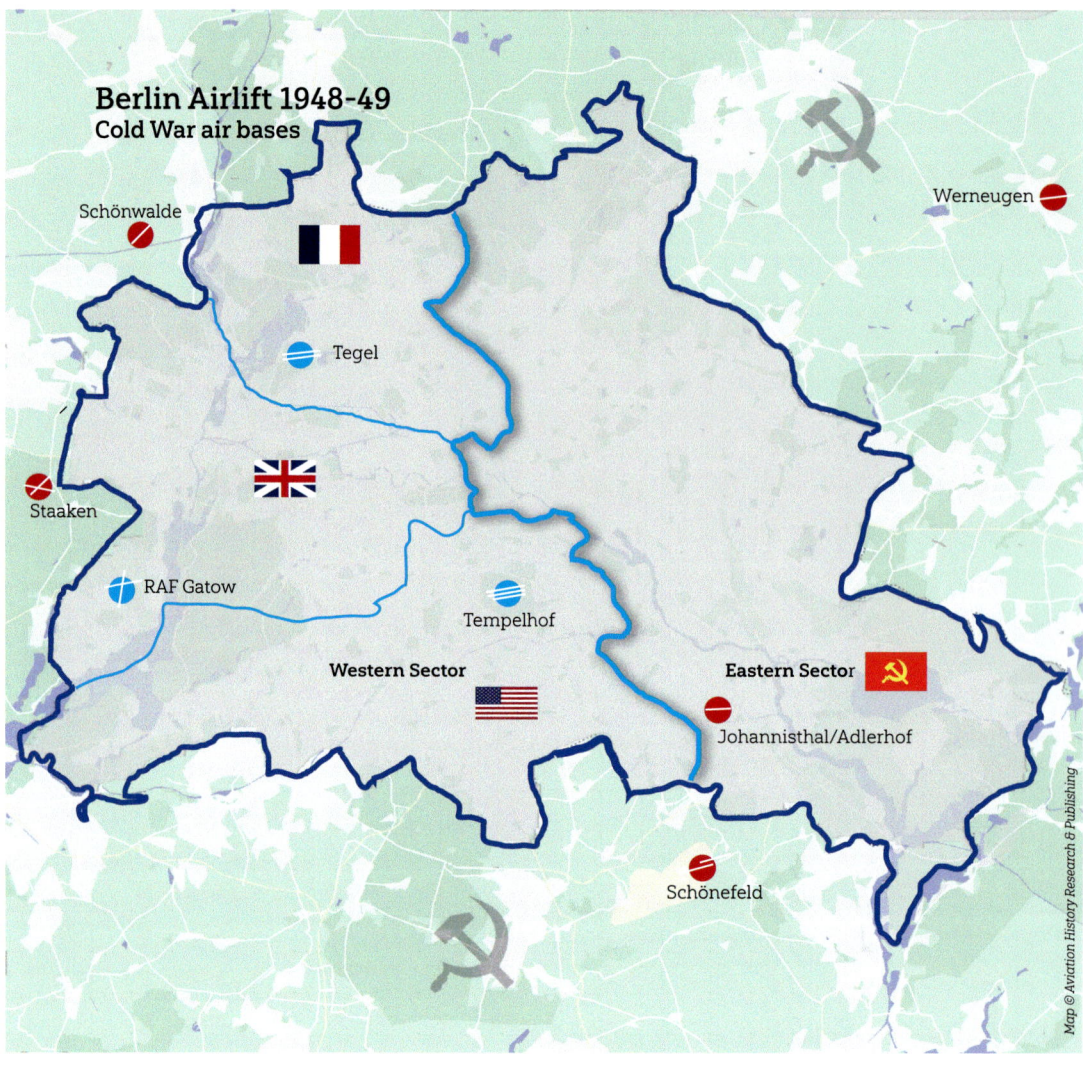

werder on the Elbe River in Hamburg. The giant flying boats of Coastal Command brought goods to Berlin and used the facilities of the British Yacht Club at Berlin-Kladow on the Havel Sea. In addition, Transport Command Hastings, Haltons, Lancastrians, and Tudors transport planes came to Germany from their bases in England.

Combined Airlift Task Force

Together, Plainfare and Vittles formed the Combined Airlift Task Force. The absence of the French in the whole operation is not surprising. After all, France had its hands full with their colonies in Indochina in 1948 (nowadays Vietnam, Cambodia, and Laos). The transport fleet of the Armee de l'Air in Indochina consisted mainly of Douglas C-47s and three-engine Amiot AAC.1 Toucans (French copy of the Junkers Ju-52). The Armee de l'Air urgently needed these aircraft to supply the French troops under increasing pressure from the Viet Minh guerrillas in Vietnam. Therefore, France's contribution to the airlift was limited and consisted of only a few Toucans and C-47s. In the German version, Ju-52s were used by Luftwaffe during World War II for landings of paratroopers and supplies to army units, of which that of the encircled German 6th Army at Stalingrad in the winter of 1942 is the best example. The German army at Stalingrad needed 700 tons of food, ammunition, and fuel daily. But no matter how grand and immersive Field Marshal Helmut Göring put on the German airlift, the Luftwaffe, with hundreds of Ju-52s and everything else that could carry cargo, proved unable to get beyond 6,591 tons of supplies, an average of 94 tons per day. It was a significant failure, leading to the surrender of the German occupying army at Stalingrad. The Ju-52 proved utterly unsuitable for a heavy and bulky airlift. The aircraft, with its characteristic ribbed "corrugated" skin, could carry only 3,307 lbs (1,500 kilograms) of cargo, which was far too little to meet the minimum daily requirements of even the French garrison.

Kremlin makes a crucial mistake

The Soviets seized on the French fiddling and the still difficult start of the airlift to smirkingly point out a failure that was dooming. That judgment, of course, was based on their own airlift performance. There was none. The Russians had yet to experience an airlift, let alone one to supply a population of 2.5 million. Although the Russian Air Force had received more than 700 Douglas C-47s via U.S. lend-lease and had around 5,000 built under license at Lisunov in Moscow, these transport aircraft had never been used for a major airlift. That requires strict logistics of goods, a doable flight schedule and air traffic control, sophisticated maintenance, and deployment of motivated pilots, mechanics, planners, loaders, unloaders, drivers, etc. And all these conditions the Soviets lacked. Logically, they reasoned that the Americans, the British, and certainly the French would probably not be able to perform something as massive as supplying a metropolis by air. This thinking may explain why the Soviets stubbornly stuck to their demands for the Western Allies to cease their monetary actions and reverse the plans for a Western Union they had decided on in London.

With the blockade of Berlin, Stalin hoped for political concessions. This assumption was based solely on his own assessment that the Western Allies would not be able to supply the population of Berlin by air. A war with the West he did not fear anyway. The Western Allies would not dare defy the Russian bear and take it out of its den. So, the blockade had to work was the view in the Kremlin. But that view turned out to be a crucial mistake.

Counterblockade hits hard

Incidentally, the Western Allies did not leave it at that. On July 26, they decided on a counterblockade banning all rail traffic in and out of the Soviet zone of Germany and halting highway freight from Western to Eastern Germany. With that, they cut off the Soviet zone from coal and steel from the Ruhr industrial region. In the weeks that followed, the Western Allies tightened their counterblockade and shut off all flow of goods from Western Germany to the East. Patrols were increased at crossing points along the length of the Bizone-frontier holding all east-bound freight on the highways. The Western counterblockade pinched the economy of the Soviet Zone sharply. Important industries were hit hard and production goals were not met. Lagging steel and metals production was blamed on lack of machinery which formerly came from Western Germany. The Red Army newspaper Tägliche Rundschau reported the steel production was running far below

The Douglas C-47 Skytrain was a cargo plane that the U.S. military deployed in large numbers during the war. It had a payload capacity of 6,000 lb. (2,722 kg). The U.S. C-47 fleet stationed in West Germany could handle nearly one hundred daily cargo delivery trips—only a fifth of what was needed to sustain Berlin. Eventually, U.S. C-47s were entirely phased out of the airlift and replaced by more potent C-54s. Photo: U.S. Air Force.

Chapter Five - Operation Vittles

> **RUSSIANS DROP LIVE BOMBS IN BERLIN PRACTICE**
>
> **Show New Bomber in Corridor Flights**
>
> BERLIN, Oct. 7.—(U.P.)—Soviet authorities announced extensive day-long maneuvers would be staged in the air lift corridors today and one British pilot reported Russian bombers dropped live bombs 10 miles from Berlin.
>
> The British pilot said he saw bombs bursting beneath Soviet plane making practice runs 10 miles north of Frohnau, northernmost suburb of the French sector of Berlin.
>
> Other pilots also reported seeing Russian bombers practicing, but said they did not see bomb bursts.
>
> Live bombing practice was not on the list of maneuvers the Russians threatened to stage. They warned they would practice anti-aircraft fire, parachute jumping, bomber fire at sleeve targets and formation and individual bomber flights from 6 A. M. to 5 P. M. in the corridor areas and over Berlin.
>
> The British-licensed newspaper Die Welt reported that from 50 to 80 four-engined Soviet bombers staged "simulated bombing raids" on Erfurt, 125 miles northwest of Frankfurt.
>
> **Show Copy of B-29**
>
> It was the first report that the Soviet Air Force was showing its copy of the American B-29 in Germany.
>
> The Soviet announcement of maneuvers was submitted to U. S., British and French authorities at the Air Safety Center at 4 A. M., only an hour before they were to start. Despite the hour, Maj. Gen. George P. Hays, deputy military governor, was notified immediately.
>
> American and British officers protested against the Soviet plans. They said the announced maneuvers violated several sections of the four-power air safety regulations. Some Western air officers regarded the announcement as the most serious threat to the air-life yet made by the Soviets.
>
> The Soviets said maneuvers would be held near Koethen, 75 miles southwest of Berlin in the American Frankfurt-Berlin corridor; near Perleberg, 75 miles west of Berlin in the British Hamburg-Berlin corridor, and at Ketzin, 20 miles west of Berlin in the British Buckeburg-Berlin corridor.
>
> **Warn of Formations**
>
> They also warned of formation flights from seven airfields along the western corridors and over Berlin.
>
> In mid-morning, after the U. S. and Britain had protested, the Russians announced additional practice —strafing in the Hamburg-Berlin corridor.
>
> The Soviet warning was pointed up by a renewed demand in the official army organ Taegliche Rundschau for Russian control over all air traffic to and from Berlin. The paper called the air lift "superfluous and too expensive."
>
> Gen. Lucius D. Clay, U. S. military governor, said an Anglo-American - French economic agreement, linking their zones in Germany, was expected to be signed within a few days. He said the agreement, "to all practical p u r p o s e s already reached," will place all exports and imports in Western Germany under a joint agency.

The Tampa Tribune, October 8, 1948.

the target and said that efforts were made to make up the difference with imports from the Soviet Union, Poland, and Czechoslovakia. The Communists shot themselves in the foot and watched as the West adequately solved the supply problems they created in Berlin.

Experience from India-China

The Kremlin strategists could have easily foreseen the U.S. capability for air supply, given the U.S. Air Force's established reputation and the successful airlift into Indo-China during World War II. In late 1942, the U.S. Army Air Force began supplying its army units in China from bases in India. Via this airlift, the American relief supplies for the Chinese nationalists led by Chiang Kai-shek in Chungking were also transported, which was anything but easy. First of all, the distances to be covered were enormous. And the route went over the high Himalayan mountains.

Despite these natural barriers, The Hump, as the airlift was called, was a great success, evidenced by statistics released by the ATC on August 1, 1945, Army Air Forces Day. President Truman had declared that day to honor the men and women of the Army Air Forces and pay tribute to those who supported the development of American air power. That day, the ATC made history by flying 1,118 return flights over the Hump, carrying 5,327 tons. Every minute and twelve seconds, an aircraft crossed the Hump; a ton of material landed in China every minute. It was all accomplished without a single accident. The peak month of The Hump Airlift was July 1945, with 71,000 tons of cargo. During the airlift, about 650,000 tons of gasoline, ammunition, other material, and men were flown over the Himalayas. And Le May brought the very man under whose command this result was achieved to Europe to head the Berlin Airlift Task Force that carried out Operation Vittles. Major General William H. Tunner, the architect of The Hump Airlift, succeeded Brigadier General Joseph Smith at the HQ Commander of the U.S. Air Forces in Europe in Wiesbaden.

The airlift gets off the ground

Smith, as temporary commander, had prepared the entire Airlift operation. Smith was a veteran with a lot of experience—at the end of the war, he was deputy chief of staff of the Eighth Air Force on Okinawa—and in a short time, he had created a management organization at Camp Lindsey, Wiesbaden, and integrated the Airlift operations at Wiesbaden, Rhein-Main, and Tempelhof. He made fundamental decisions, including the sixty-five percent standard for minimum aircraft commissioning, and stipulated that every aircraft in operation had to make three round trips daily. Under Smith's brief leadership, a centrally controlled Air Traffic Center was established, and the operation was expanded to include the RAF bases Fassberg and Celle. By the second half of July, the airlift showed considerable improvement in organization and efficiency. Headquarters at Camp Lindsey, Wiesbaden, had been expanded and commanded the entire operation. The 60th Troop Carrier Group at Wiesbaden and the 61st Troop Carrier Group at Rhein-Main replaced their C-47s with the much larger C-54 Skymasters. MATS flew these aircraft to Germany from MATS units in Alaska, Panama, Hawaii, Japan, Guam, and the United States. Smith's team had calculated that the required minimum of 4,500 tons of cargo per day to Berlin over thirty days would need a fleet of 899 C-47s with 39,706 return flights. The same monthly tonnage could be flown by 178 C-54s, which would get the job done with 13,800 return flights—using six million fewer gallons of gasoline and requiring less maintenance.[74] Deployment of the four-engined C-54 would be much more efficient for the airlift.

The first C-54 arrived at Rhein-Main in the morning of July 1, and the first Skymaster cleared for Tempelhof just over ten hours later. By July 2, seventeen of the big birds had reached Rhein-Main. Four days later, thirty-six C-54s aircraft had arrived from Alaska, the Panama Canal Zone, and Hawaii and were attached to Rhein-Main Air Base.[75] As additional

C-54s arrived, the C-47s returned to their home bases, leaving their crews behind. Rhein-Main Air Base exclusively became a C-54 hub, while Wiesbaden retained a mix of C-54s and C-47s. That situation remained until, by October 1, the complete Airlift fleet of C-47s was replaced by C-54s. With the arrival of the Skymasters, the average daily delivery rate began to climb, tripling from just over 500 tons per day at the end of June. On July 31, Operation Vittles delivered 1,719.5 tons of cargo. With 122 roundtrips, the C-54s had delivered 1,072 tons, while with 200 roundtrips, the C-47s had delivered 647.1 tons. The British Plainfare airlift delivered 1,437 tons on the same day. Vittles and Plainfare combined delivered a total of 3,156.5 tons, still well below the 4,500 tons per day required in Berlin.[76]

Tunner averts shambles

On July 28, William Tunner's personal C-54G serial 45-549 touched down on Wiesbaden Air Force Base. The transport specialist known as "Willie the Whip" came to lead what would become the world's largest airlift ever. The airlift was just four weeks on when Tunner was briefed about the problems in these early weeks of the project. The use of different types of aircraft with different cruising speeds gave the biggest headache to American traffic controllers. The C-54 was faster than the C-47, and

Douglas C-54 aircraft from U.S. Air Force MATS units are being unloaded of their cargo at Tempelhof during the Berlin Airlift. Involvement of the U.S. Navy began in October 1948, when two Navy MATS squadrons (VR6 from Honolulu and VR8 from Guam), equipped with a total of 24 R5Ds (Navy version of the DC-4), were deployed to Rhein-Main Air Base and also took part in the Airlift Task Force. Photo: U.S. Air Force.

Chapter Five - **Operation Vittles**

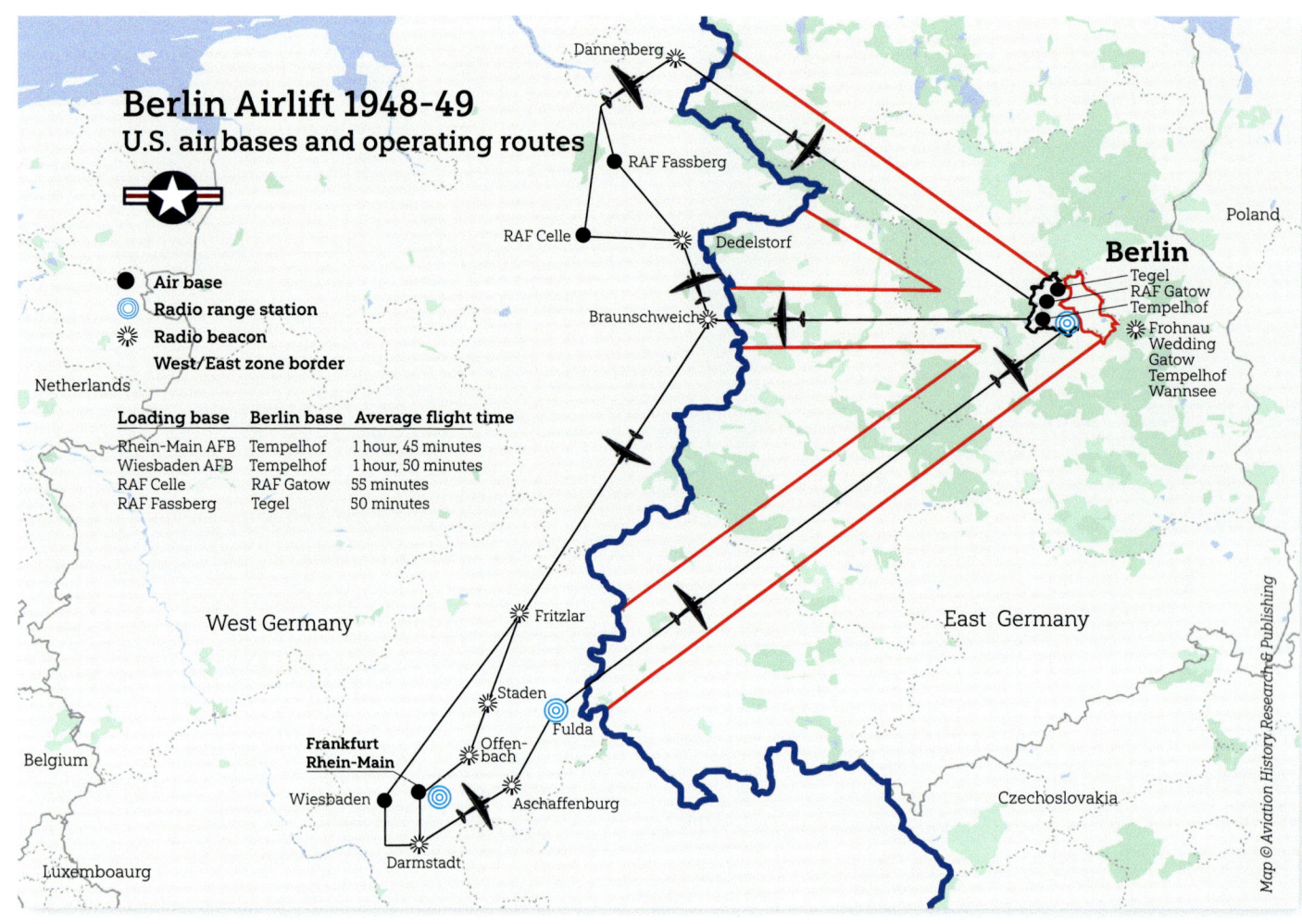

Three air corridors connected the airfields in Berlin with those in the British and American occupation zones. U.S. aircraft operated from two bases in the American zone, Rhein-Main and Wiesbaden. Initially, the C-47 Skytrain was the workhorse of the airlift. From August 1948 onwards, it was gradually replaced by the Douglas C-54 Skymaster. These four-engined cargo planes could carry a load of 10 tons (9,072 kg), almost three times the payload of a C-47. By the end of 1948, 225 C-54s were operational in the daily airlift schedule: 95 from Rhein-Main, 26 from Wiesbaden, 46 from RAF Celle, and 58 from RAF Fassberg.

to avoid overtaking them on the way, the C-54s always had to start first. Only when a group of C-54s was on the way could the C-47s start. As more aircraft began to take part in Vittles, the problems for the Air Lift Task Force grew.

Vittles could quickly become shambles unless an efficient traffic system was introduced. The situation was made painfully clear to Tunner during his inspection flight on August 13. That day, Berlin had its worst storm in thirty years. Tunner had left Wiesbaden that morning in fair weather, but once his C-54 arrived at Berlin, the conditions became horrible, and the radar was washed out. Two transport aircraft crashed one after the other at Tempelhof, completely blocking the runway. At the same time, another couldn't find the runway and landed on

the provisional runway just under construction. Tunner's C-54 was 28th in a long queue of transport aircraft waiting to begin their approach. Action was needed to prevent more accidents. General Tunner ordered all aircraft waiting to land at Tempelhof back to their bases in West Germany. After this incident at Tempelhof, a furious Tunner demanded that a new system for traffic control to and from Berlin be worked out and implemented.

A new traffic control system

The unique feature of the new traffic control system was the use of different flight altitudes. A vertical separation of five hundred feet was introduced, which was sufficient to allow far more aircraft to use the air corridors at the same time. Moreover, the southern corridor was used exclusively for traffic from Wiesbaden and Rhein-Main to Berlin under the new system. The northern corridor carried traffic from Celle and Fassberg and the increasing RAF traffic. The central corridor was only used by traffic returning to the American bases in West Germany. These measures considerably increased air safety, which was Tunner's aim.

Henceforth, transport aircraft took off from one of the four American airfields at intervals of at least three minutes. A flight could, for example, start at Rhein-Main where flying continued around the clock seven days a week. The pilot of any given C-54 called the tower shortly before take-off and told the traffic controller its call sign for the flight: "Big Easy" followed by the number of its hardstand and the last three numbers of the plane's serial number. Westward the call sign changed to "Big Willy." The traffic controller gave the exact flying altitude for the flight through the corridor and the time at which the aircraft must pass the Fulda radio beacon. Fulda lay almost in the middle of the entrance to the southernmost corridor and formed an ideal starting point.

The horizontal separation was precisely fifteen minutes in the first months of the airlift. Later, this time became constantly shorter when traffic increased until there were only three minutes between aircraft. After approximately forty minutes of flight through the corridor, the aircraft began its approach to Tempelhof. Once the aircraft reached a height of 2,000 feet, Berlin Traffic Control switched over to Jigsaw, the code name for Tempelhof's Ground Control Approach (GCA).

As soon as the GCA had the concerned aircraft on the radar screen, it was guided to the correct position in the circuit and directed to the runway. About 6 miles (10 kilometers) out from Tempelhof, the final controller took over from GCA. Landing at Tempelhof, in the center of the city, was complicated and dangerous because of the high buildings on both sides of the flight path.

At night or in bad weather, the final controller talked the pilots down through this risky last phase. He constantly corrected every course deviation, and the pilot had to carry out his instructions to the letter. The "Take-over-and-land" order came around fifty feet (fifteen meters) from the runway, after which the pilot could put the aircraft down on the ground.[77] If he missed the first time, he had to fly back, with

Above, a Big Easy C-54 roars past a Ground-Controlled Approach (GCA) unit on take-off from Rhein-Main Air Base. The radio call sign "Big Easy," the code for eastbound C-54s landing in Berlin, became perhaps the most recognized phrase on the radio during the Berlin Airlift. Below: Mission briefing at Rhein-Main. Photos: U.S. Air Force.

Chapter Five - Operation Vittles

The bustling daily air traffic at Tempelhof drew the interest of many spectators. In the photo, youths are seen watching the takeoff of a reconnaissance version of a Boeing B-17.
Photo: NARA.

Douglas RB-26C Invader 44-35914 Hot Lips from the 45th Reconnaissance Squadron parked on the visitors' platform of RAF Northolt near London. The Invaders of the 45th operated mostly at night and were painted all black, with the registration in red
Photo: Les Vowles/ABPIC.

his load, to the base from where he had come. In the extremely tight traffic control schedule with an aircraft landing every three minutes, there was no second chance. The establishment of GCA units along with high intensity landing lights at Tempelhof and Gatow and other navigational aids enabled the C-54 Skymasters to operate in all but the worst weather.

Covert flights

Another issue was the navigation in the narrow corridors. The American pilots were not used to flying under stringent conditions, such as in narrow corridors. It frequently happened that aircraft ended up outside the limits of the corridors, missed a radio beacon, or got lost. Bad weather and malfunctions of instruments were often the cause. But fatigue and sheer boredom that compromised alertness also played a role. And while the Soviets already had great difficulty with the Western Allies using the corridors, straying from them was a thorn in their side, especially since they could suspect that among the regular cargo traffic, there were also Big Easy planes flying in the corridors carrying special equipment, such as cameras and radio receivers, instead of potatoes, milk, or coal.

These covert aircraft came from Fürstenfeldbruck Air Base. At this Bavarian base near Munich, Boeing RB-29 spy planes were regularly deployed between 1947 and 1948. In the fall 1948, the 45th Reconnaissance Squadron operated from there.[78] The 45th RS went to Fürstenfeldbruck in March 1947 from Fürth Air Base near Nürnberg as part of the 10th Reconnaissance Group.[79] It was a composite unit of twenty-one Douglas A-26 and FA-26s, North American F-6s (reconnaissance version of the P-51 Mustang), and Boeing B-17s and its primary task was photomapping. During the Berlin Airlift, the 45th became a secretive unit actively involved in USAFE covert flights.

About fifteen A-26 twin-engined light bomber and ground attack aircraft[80] had been converted to RB-26s and equipped with three sizable cameras: a 2-inch and a 24-inch camera in the bomb bay for vertical photography on 9x9-inch film and a forward-facing 24-inch oblique camera in the nose for panoramic photographs on 9 x 18-inch film.[81] The RB-17s came from the 10th Reconnaissance Group that briefly operated the type from Fürstenfeldbruck until the unit and its assigned 1st and 160th Reconnaissance Squadrons were disbanded in June 1947 and left for the USA, leaving the B-17s behind. The 45th RS remained at Fürstenfeldbruck, and in May 1948, it became part of the 86th Composite Wing, also stationed at Fürstenfeldbruck. When the 86th and its three fighter squadrons moved

By July 1, 1948, the addition of C-54s to the fleet marked the beginning of a heavy transport fleet, which by January 1, 1949, had grown to 201 USAF C-54s and 24 Navy R-5Ds aircraft. The photo shows a row of five C-54s waiting to take-off at Rhein-Main Air Base. Photo: U.S. Air Force.

to Neubiberg Air Base just south of Munich, the 45th became part of the 7300th Air Force Composite Wing attached to the 36th Fighter Wing.[82]

The 45th was redesignated Tactical Reconnaissance Squadron, Night Photographic (TRS) in July 1948 and its focus shifted to the Soviet occupation zone in eastern Germany; the air corridors were ideal for conducting night photoreconnaissance. And not only of the military activities on the ground in the corridors, but also far beyond. With side-looking cameras, a large area could be photographed in detail. Furthermore, the Americans and the British were interested in picking up electronic signals.

Just as the B-17s of the 10th RG in 1946 provided proof of radar used by the Yugoslav Army, with ELINT ferret flights in the Berlin corridors, USAFE got a good picture of Russian radar technology and the Red Army's readiness.

Only at night

The RB-17s and RB-26s were covertly inserted into the airlift traffic under cover of the regular meteorologic reconnaissance flights of the 7169th Weather Reconnaissance Squadron based at Oberpfaffenhofen, which flew B-17s from Wiesbaden too.[83] These aircraft flew with every airlift block and were equipped to transmit weather reports on icing conditions and extreme turbulence in the air corridors. The covert flights took place only at night. The RB-17s and RB-26s never landed at Tempelhof; it would quickly reveal their true identity, which could lead to a diplomatic row or worse. To avoid landing in Berlin, they would declare "an emergency" or "landing gear problems" that necessitated an immediate return to the Western Zones.[84]

The cat-and-mouse game between the Americans and the Russians culminated when the Soviets announced in October that the Russian Air Force in Eastern Germany had been ordered to force down any aircraft exceeding the twenty-mile confines of the corridors leading into and out of Berlin. With so many aircraft in the corridors daily, the likelihood of that happening was relatively high with all its consequences.

The 45th TRS continued flying covert missions until the squadron was disbanded in March 1949. Its RB-26s transferred to the 7499th Air Force Squadron, that already operated the RB-17s of the 10th RG. The 7499th Air Force

Major General William Henry Tunner (1906-1983) was Air Inspector of the U.S. Air Transport Command (ATC) when he was called to lead Operation Vittles in July 1948. Tunner was known for his vast experience in leading large-scale military air transport operations. Photo: U.S. Air Force.

Aviation History Research & Publishing   61

Chapter Five - Operation Vittles

Squadron was redesignated Composite Squadron two months later and from that moment on the squadron gradually expanded its covert aircraft fleet with innocent-looking C-47s, C-54s, and C-97s. They would form the nucleus of USAFE's covert reconnaissance mission during the Cold War. Still operating from Fürstenfeldbruck, but as soon as space became available at Wiesbaden in August 1950, the secret circus moved there, close to USAFE headquarters and the corridors to Berlin.

Two airfields are not enough

While air traffic control was a challenge, the runways and taxiways at Tempelhof and Gatow presented even more problems. They were suffering greatly under the weight of increasingly heavy transport planes. The infrastructure at Gatow nor at Tempelhof was suited for this kind of traffic. As early as June, repair crews had to work regularly to fill the holes in the concrete and repair the pierced steel plates. At Tempelhof, a team of two hundred German workers was permanently at ready with shovels and wheelbarrows full of sand and asphalt to quickly repair the damage. This happened between flight operations; as soon as a heavily loaded plane landed, the workers rushed onto the runway and hurriedly went to work until a few minutes later, the whistle sounded again as a signal of an approaching plane. As soon as it had passed, they ran with tools onto the runway. And this went on all the time, twenty-four hours a day, day in and day out. But the repairs were all only temporary. By the end of June, the runway at Tempelhof had deteriorated so quickly that it was about to break down rapidly under the impact of the heavily-loaded C-47s.

The Skymasters risked even greater damage. It was decided to construct a second asphalt and pierced steel plank runway south of the existing one. German contractors began work on July 8.[85] American enlisted personnel operated the heavy machinery, including graders and bulldozers, while German civilians, both men and women, did the rest by hand. The rubble for the base foundation was readily available thanks to the Allied bombing campaign in World War II.

All other material had to be flown in from the U.S. occupation zone, which added significantly to the airlift burden.[86] Meanwhile, the existing runway was maintained around the clock. By August, construction on the south runway at Tempelhof was well along, but it was already apparent to Airlift Task Force planners that with more C-54s on the way, a third runway was necessary. Thus, by the end of the month, construction began on another runway to the north of the main runway. However, even with additional runways, Gatow and Tempelhof were too cramped to meet the projected demands of the airlift.

The two airfields could cope with the number of take-offs and landings, but the infrastructure was not built to cope with thousands of tons of freight each day. A third airfield was desperately needed. A site was found in the Wedding suburb in the French sector, which had been used during the war as a training ground for Luftwaffe air defense divisions and now lay waste.

Clay puts pressure on

The British were rather skeptical about the benefits of the third airfield, telling the Americans that it would considerably increase traffic

The U.S. Airlift Task Force recorded at least 733 incidents in the air corridors involving the Russians. In most cases, Russian Yak-3 fighters conducted mock attacks, with their pilots managing to startle American pilots by flying straight through formations of transports at high speed. This "buzzing" caused great confusion and panic among the pilots, which considerably increased the danger of collisions in the air. Russian sabotage activities increased both in number and severity as the airlift grew in size and intensity. Western radio frequencies were jammed, and chaff (aluminum strips that disrupted radar systems) were sown. Searchlights were shone on aircraft on night flights. The photo shows a Russian Yak-3 fighter similar to those operated by the Red Army in East Germany after World War II. Photo: VVS.

and serviced at Wiesbaden Air Base for another flight to Berlin during Operation Vittles. Left 42-72452 "432" and right 45-629 "403." At the far right is just visible Fairchild C-82A 45-57791, which at that time was part of the 7165th Composite Group at Wiesbaden. Photo: U.S. Air Force.

in the air corridors. According to the Americans, this was a minor problem. They had calculated that if the building started on September 5, the airfield could be operational in February 1949. "Much too long," Clay told General Le May. "I don't accept the opening estimate for Tegel," said The-Great-Uncompromiser Clay. Ultimately, dedication ceremonies at Tegel took place on October 29, and operations began on November 5, just three months after construction began.

Work on this ambitious plan began directly. Rubble from bombed-out buildings in the neighborhood and stones from several unused railways were used in the construction. In a short while, 17,000 German workers—hired for DM1.20 per hour plus a warm meal[87] – worked in three shifts around the clock. Tegel required a monumental effort. Construction began on August 5 and included a 5,500-feet (1,676 meters) runway of brick rubble with an asphalt surface, over one million square feet of the apron, 6,020 feet (1,835 meters) of taxiway, 4,400 feet (1,341 meters) of an access road, and 2,750 feet (838 meters) of access railroad. Furthermore, administrative, operations, and support buildings, a control tower, a fire station and ground control approach (GCA) radar sites were needed.[88] One problem was that the necessary construction equipment was not found in Berlin. So, the large machines were broken down into sections at Rhein-Main and Wiesbaden and flown to Tempelhof in Fairchild C-82 Packet transport aircraft, of which five were assigned to the airlift. They were deployed of the 316th Troop Carrier Group, Greenfield AFB, Mississippi. During the airlift, they were part of the 12th Troop Carrier Squadron based at Wiesbaden. The Packet's advantage lay in its wide fuselage and access through the rear, which made it excellent for hauling unwieldy cargo, such as heavy, bulky equipment and automobiles.

Huge amount of rubble

A giant Douglas C-74 Globemaster I had to be used to transport one enormous pulverizer even though it was broken down into several pieces. At Tempelhof the pulverizer was put back together again and moved to the construction site where it was used to process the huge amount of rubble needed for the runways. The ground where the runway and the taxiway had to be constructed was undulating which meant that in several places the foundations of the 5,500-feet (1,676 meters) runway were one and a half meters thick. Tegel air base was literally pounded out of the ground.

Chapter Five - **Operation Vittles**

The organization of the United States Air Forces in Europe was relatively small. As of January 1, 1949, the organization had 47,392 personnel assigned and 368 aircraft (B-17, B-26, C-45, C-47, C-54, C-82, F-47, F-80, L-5, RB-26, and T-6) at nine permanent installations (and one in Austria) and major command holdings at approximately 15 others.
In September 1948, USAF established Burtonwood Air Force Depot. This depot, based at RAF Burtonwood, Cheshire, UK, was responsible for stocking supplies in addition to those stored at Erding. Burtonwood also became the major depot for the Mutual Defense Assistance Program (MDAP) supplies.

The airfield was just about ready on November 6 to receive its first ceremonial flight; a Douglas C-54 Skymaster brought a celebrational load of cheese.[89] From the middle of November, Tegel was operational and could handle transport aircraft.

Allied co-operation

Their occupation zone gave the British significant advantages. The zone was relatively flat, while the Americans in the southern corridor had to fly over Rhön with mountains of 2,625 feet high (800 meters) while returning traffic to Wiesbaden had to cross the Taunus with peaks reaching 2,950 feet (900 meters). The weather in the British zone in the north of Germany tended to be milder with less fog. More significantly, the British had shorter distances to fly. The southern corridor was 186 miles (300 kilometers), half as long as the northern corridor, enabling British aircraft to make more daily trips to Berlin. The U.S. Vittles operation and its British counterpart Plainfare were functionally combined into the Combined Air Lift Task Force (CALTF) with General Tunner in overall command. The absence of the French in the whole operation was noteworthy. For a while, the French, who did not have an airfield at their disposal in their occupation zone, operated from British Wunsdorf and flew to Gatow with their French-built Ju-52 tri-engined aircraft. But even the tiny French contribution to the airlift came to an early end because of language issues (communications during the airlift were in English) and operational problems (the Toucans were way too slow). The French had to withdraw from the airlift. The French occupation force made its most outstanding contribution to the Berlin airlift by allowing the construction of Tegel in its zone.

After Tegel opened, the French garrison made one more contribution. A 200-feet (61 meters) radio tower belonging to Berliner Rundfunk but under Soviet control, provided a serious landing hazard at the new field. General Jean Ganeval had unsuccessfully requested a few times to remove the radio towers. He warned the Soviets that if the towers were not moved, he would remove them himself. Failing to receive a response, Ganeval, on December 16, ordered his gendarmes to blow up the tower. The Russians called it an "Act of Violence" and were outraged. The Communist-controlled Berlin press branded the destruction of the tower as an act of cultural barbarism carried out at American command and as a disgrace to France.[90]

Easter parade breaks all records

In April and May 1949, when Operation Vittles was at its height, 336 transport aircraft were involved in the airlift, of which 230 (225 Douglas C-54/RD5s and 5 Fairchild C-82 Packets) were used for flights through the air corridors to Berlin. The rest was used to provision the American bases in West Germany that were involved in Vittles, for bringing in spare parts, etc. In 1948, during the first month of the airlift, American transports brought around 41,000 tons of food, fuel, coal, etc., to Berlin. This took 8,100 flights, most of them with C-47s.

The effort of hundreds of pilots and thousands of military and civilians involved in the airlift was enormous and was best illustrated by the "Easter Parade" of April 16, 1949. On that one day, the CALTF delivered nearly 13,000 tons of provisions with 1,398 flights. The stream was so great that an aircraft landed almost once a minute at one of the three Berlin airfields. The effort in May 1949 was so great, that more than 192,000 tons of cargo were flown to isolated Berlin. It took over 19,300 return flights. In this record month, the British contribution to the airlift was also significant, with 58,000 tons realized with 8,300 return flights. The British/American cooperation ran like a well-oiled machine, and from a logistical standpoint, the prospects were excellent.

The C-124 meets Tunner's criteria

At the height of the airlift, the CALTF was flying out of nine airfields and delivering to three. With a fleet of Douglas C-74s, the airlift could have delivered 8,000 tons of cargo daily, operating out of two bases and delivering

On August 11, 1948, at Westover AFB, Massachusetts, Douglas C-74 Globemaster I serial 42-65414, part of the 521st Air Transport Group at Brookley Air Force Base, Alabama, prepared for a special mission to Germany. The C-74 departed for Rhein-Main within a few days, carrying eighteen replacement C-54 engines. On August 14, after a flight via Lajes, the American support post on the Azores, the aircraft arrived at the West German air base. Before its return to the United States on September 21, the C-74 delivered 445.6 tons of cargo in twenty-five trips, usually out of Rhein-Main and Kaufbeuren, with an average of 17.82 tons per trip, proving itself as tremendously superior to the C-54. Tunner's office had calculated that 68 C-74s could do the work of 180 C-54s moving the minimum 13,500 tons of daily freight in only 5,400 flights, rather than the 13,800 needed with the C-54s. Unfortunately, there were only fourteen C-74s built, and the plane proved too heavy for the Tempelhof and Gatow runways, which were only provisional and consisted mainly of pierced steel planking. An unladen Globemaster weighed twice as much as a C-54 full to the rim with coal. Multiple landings, in quick succession with heavily laden C-74s, would have destroyed the runways at Tempelhof. Photo: Douglas.

to only one. With additional air bases and two in Berlin, Tunner believed that he could deliver over 24,000 tons of cargo daily,[91] or more than five times the minimum the city required. And all of this could be done at a substantially reduced cost. The Douglas C-124 Globemaster II, the vastly improved successor of the C-74, could lift an amazing thirty-one tons and was already on its way. The C-124 would fully meet Tunner's criteria. A glimpse of the future was given to the public on May 4, 1949, when a Boeing YC-97 Stratocruiser landed on Tempelhof. The transport version of the Boeing B-29 bomber could carry twenty-five tons, and it demonstrated its capacity during tests in May. It flew twenty-three missions, delivering 444.8 tons of cargo to Berlin.[92]

The Western Allies' response to Communist aggression was a logistical operation, unprecedented under Tunner's leadership. Berlin was not abandoned, despite the threat of war and the realization that the huge Russian army was easily able to advance all the way to the Rhine/IJssel River in a short period of time. Continuation of the airlift prevented war. Besides, there was always the atomic bomb. And the Americans possessed it and the aircraft to drop the bomb. However, these aircraft remained at their Roswell base in New Mexico throughout the crisis, albeit on twenty-four-hour alert.

A pact against armed aggression

Soviet leader Joseph Stalin must also have understood that the blockade was a major failure. It was a political move, but it turned out quite badly for the Soviet Union. Berlin would not turn to communism; that much was clear. The Western Allies would not retreat. Diversionary tactics by the Soviets did not have much effect. The Iron Curtain countries had, of course, noticed the failure of the much-publicized takeover of Berlin. Realizing that Stalin was going to retreat severely strained their confidence in the Communist leader, who began to withdraw restrictions without demanding large compensatory concessions. Stalin had failed to block the forming of the Western Union or the Brussels Pact, which was signed by Belgium, France, Luxembourg, the Netherlands, and the United Kingdom before the blockade and which served as the founding Treaty of the Western European Union (WEU). The blockade of Berlin and the threat of war pressed the plans for the defense of the West and negotiations for a North Atlantic treaty forward. Quite the opposite of what the Soviet Union had anticipated.

On March 15, 1949, the five Brussels Treaty Powers, Canada and the United States, formally invited Denmark, Iceland, Italy, Norway, and Portugal to adhere to the Treaty. On March 31, the Soviet Union presented a memorandum to the twelve prospective signatories claiming that the Treaty was contrary to the United Nations Charter. The twelve countries delivered their reply to Russia two days later, stating on half an A4-paper that the text of the Treaty was the best answer to Soviet allegations since it showed beyond a shadow of a doubt that the Alliance was not aimed against any nation or group of nations, but only against armed aggression.

The West didn't give

"Perhaps we should kick them out," suggested the Communist leader Joseph Stalin in March 1948. One year later, he must have realized that none of the conditions to lift the blockade were realized. The Allies remained loyal to the people of Berlin and did not leave the divided city; the DM was introduced, bringing Germany's recovery closer more quickly, and the Atlantic military alliance came to pass. Above all, and this perhaps affected Stalin the most, the Soviet Union was economically hit hard by the counterblockade of the Western Allies. The airlift broke the blockade and showed the West's determination not to give in. The Soviets, too, came to realize that, thanks to the airlift of the Berlin blockade, they would not achieve the desired political effect.

On May 12, 1949, Stalin lifted the blockade. The Soviets had lost the severe first skirmish of the Cold War.

March 1949 began with high winds and heavy snow at most airlift bases, but operations continued on a near-normal schedule. The photo shows the loading and refueling of C-54G 45-527 with code "440" on its tail. After the Berlin Airlift, this Skymaster was used for test purposes as JC-54G. In 1970, it was transferred to the Fuerza Aerea Colombiana (FAC) as FAC-694 based at the Colombian Air Base of Palanquero, assigned to the Comando Aereo de Transporte Militar. After fifty-three years of service, it was withdrawn from use in April 1998.
Photo: U.S. Air Force.

Chapter Six

U.S. Deterrence

The North American B-45A Tornado was a four-engined jet bomber that made its first flight on February 24, 1947. It was the first operational jet bomber of the USAF and was classified as a light tactical bomber. It was also the first jet bomber capable of carrying an atomic bomb. The B-45 had a top speed of 566 mph (911 km/h), while its service ceiling was 46,000 feet (14,000 meters). Likewise, its combat range was impressive: 1,192 miles (1,918 kilometers). From bases in East Anglia, England, the bomber could reach Soviet targets in the Baltics, Belarus, Ukraine, and Romania. Modified with a 1,200 gallons (4,542 liters) fuel tank in the aft bomb bay, it could reach even further. It entered service in April 1948, when 22 Tornados went to the 47th Bombardment Group at Barksdale AFB, Louisiana. In its heyday, the B-45 was essential to the U.S. defense strategy, performing the strategically critical deterrence mission for several years during the late 1940s and the early 1950s. During the early years of the Cold War, many B-45s were converted for reconnaissance operations. Photo: U.S. Air Force.

During 1948, defense developments in the U.S. slowly but surely picked up speed. After World War II, demobilization had occurred at a record pace, with the result that in 1948 the U.S. armed forces were a mere pittance of what they had been less than three years earlier. In Europe, the U.S. air power was in poor shape and no longer a big deal. American forces had left England, where hundreds of airfields had once been used by the then USAAF. And in continental Europe, the Americans had bases only in occupied territories. The air bases were easily possible in Germany, Austria, and Italy because the U.S. was an occupying force there. The U.S. did not need complicated diplomatic negotiations with governments to obtain permission to use these bases. Instead of permanent stationing, the USAF opted for short-term training deployments. And because tensions in Europe were rising considerably, B-29 deployments to Germany began in 1947, first to Giebelstadt and later to Fürstenfeldbruck. These deployments to Germany took place under the code name Sunfast. Deployments also resumed in the Far East. The shortage of 100/130 octane gasoline was largely solved so that from February 1948, the squadron rotations continued to Yokota Air Base. The European and Far Eastern deployments usually consisted of a squadron of ten B-29s and two Douglas C-54s for escort. An RB-29 from the 311th Air Division (Reconnaissance) also always accompanied them. The northern and southern Atlantic routes were utilized on European en-route and return flights. Units staging through MacDill Air Force Base, Florida, flew to Europe via Lajes Field, Azores. Those staging through Westover Air Force Base, Massachusetts, flew via either Goose Bay Air Base, Labrador, or Keflavik Air Base, Iceland. The B-29s going to the Far East took the Pacific route. The staging was at Castle Field Air Force Base, California, with a refueling stop at Hickham Air Force Base, Hawaii, before hopping to Bucholz Army Airfield, Kwajalein Atoll, Marshall Islands, where the B-29s were prepared for the next hop to Andersen Air Force Base on Guam. Then they went on to Yokota Air Base near Tokyo. Notably, the 393rd Composite Squadron of the 509th Bombardment Group, responsible for the atomic attack on Hiroshima, was the first unit stationed at Yokota in February 1948, temporarily, but under the operational control of the U.S. Far East Air Force (FEAF). The 509th Bombardment Group also conducted a series of four aircraft to SAC's air base at Shemya Island on the Alaskan Aleutians in the Bering Strait in the North Pacific. The first flight of nuclear Silverplate B-29s bombers arrived at the strategically located air base just 500 miles (805 kilometers) away from the Russian peninsula of Kamchatka on June 14, 1948. The four-aircraft flights, which also involved the 7th and 97th Bombardment Groups, continued throughout the summer and ceased in November 1948.[93] The four-plane flights that also involved the 7th and 97th Bombardment Groups continued through the summer and were suspended in November 1948.

Bomber training in Germany

Apparently, Washington did not want to go that far in Europe, because the temporary B-29 units based there were all non-atomic. In Europe, the B-29s were not for deterrence but for training. At least, that was the official line. From the beginning of Operation Sunfast in July 1947 until June 1948, ten B-29 units were temporarily assigned to the United States Air Forces in Europe (USAFE). And although the B-29s were only for training in Germany, according to US-AFE, the B-29's reputation as an atomic bomber did cause diplomatic concerns. The failure of some European nations to grant clearances for operational flights limited the effective scope of SAC. The B-29 rotational squadrons performed familiarization flights and aerial reviews over Western Europe, as well as radar bombing and navigational training flights. Some units flew missions to Dhahran, Saudi Arabia.

SAC's plan was to send entire groups (three squadrons totaling thirty B-29s) on rotations to Europe. The intention was for those group rotations to last ninety days, but it didn't get that far in 1947 or 1948. As part of the new ninety-day program, the Strategic Air Command scheduled the 301st Bombardment Group to leave their base Smoky Hill Air Force Base, Kansas, on April 5, the 98th Group in July, and the 307th Group in October. However, because USAFE did not have the personnel and facilities to accommodate a whole B-29 group, the 301st Group, which initiated the program in the middle of April, could stay in Germany only for one week.[94] The program was then abruptly terminated at Headquarters United States Air Force direction, when two squadrons of the 301st Group (the 32nd and 353rd) returned to the United States on April 20. One squadron (the 352nd) remained in Germany at Fürstenfeldbruck as part of the squadron rotation program. It was not until July 1948, shortly after the beginning of the Berlin Airlift, that the program for the rotation of groups to Europe was successfully established. The initiative

The Boeing B-47, shown here as the XB-47 prototype 46-065 during roll out from its hangar on December 12, 1947, in Seattle, was an essential part of the United States' nuclear deterrent from the 1950s until the early 1960s. The last B-47 (an EB-47E model - serial 52-0412) went out of service in 1977, forty years after roll-out. Its swept-wing design and six 7,200-pound-thrust General Electric J-47 axial-flow turbojets gave the bomber fighter-like performances with a top speed of 607 mph (977 km/h) and a service ceiling of 40,500 feet (12,300 meters). With underwing tanks, the B-47 had a maximum range of 4,990 miles (8,031 kilometers), and with a combat radius of 2,013 miles (3,240 kilometers), it could, from its UK-bases like RAF Greenham Common, reach Russian places like Saratov on the Volga River. The Stratojet, of which 2,032 were built, could carry a nuclear load of 25,000 lb (11,340 kg); for instance, 2 Mk15 nuclear bombs each of 3.8 megatons yield. Photo: Boeing Company.

Chapter Six - U.S. Deterrence

SAC Operation Sunfast - Bombardment units rotated to Europe July 1947 - June 1948

Dates*	Unit	Base
1947		
July 3-19	97th Bombardment Group, Smoky Hill, Kansas	Giebelstadt
July 21 - August 9	307th Bombardment Group (2 squadrons), MacDill, Florida and 28th Bombardment Group (1 squadron), Rapid City, South Dakota	Giebelstadt
August 12 - September 1	43rd Bombardment Group (2 squadrons), Davis-Monthan, Arizona	Giebelstadt
September 2 - september 20	7th Bombardment Group, Fort Worth, Texas	Giebelstadt
November 15 - December 15	28th Bombardment Group (1 squadron), Rapid City, South Dakota	Giebelstadt
December 12 - January 28	307th Bombardment Group (1 squadron), MacDill, Florida	Fürstenfeldbruck
1948		
January 22 - March 2	28th Bombardment Group (1 squadron), Rapid City, South Dakota	Fürstenfeldbruck
February 25 - April 7	7th Bombardment Group (1 squadron), Carswell, Texas	Fürstenfeldbruck
April 13 - May 27	301st Bombardment Group (1 squadron), Smoky Hill, Kansas	Fürstenfeldbruck
May 23 - June 14	301st Bombardment Group (1 squadron), Smoky Hill, Kansas	Fürstenfeldbruck
June 3 - August 12	301st Bombardment Group (1 squadron), Smoky Hill, Kansas	Fürstenfeldbruck
SAC Berlin blockade response		
July 2 - August 12	301st Bombardment Group (2 squadrons), Smoky Hill, Kansas	Fürstenfeldbruck

* Arrival date and date last aircraft returned. Source: SAC Historical Study No. 61

came from the British—on June 26, 1948, to be precise. Ernest Bevin, the British uncompromising foreign minister, told the American ambassador in London that the airlift would give the Western Allies time for negotiations. But he also told the U.S. to send heavy bombers so the Soviets would understand that things were serious. Through diplomatic channels, the message was relayed to General Clay in Berlin. The next day Clay sent a request to Washington to expand the contingent B-29s in Germany. Expansion of the deployment at Fürstenfeldbruck to the size of a group was obvious. SAC immediately ordered the group's other two squadrons to Goose Bay Air Base, Labrador, to prepare for immediate deployment to Germany. The squadrons were on three-hour alert, and for the first time since the end of the war, SAC could now show in practice that it could deploy quickly in a crisis.

B-29s within striking distance

The first increment of the two-squadron flights arrived in Germany on June 29, within forty-five hours after being alerted. By July 2, all but two B-29s of the two squadrons were in place at their base in Bavaria. The two squadrons stayed there only a little more than a month. During the entire time the unit was stationed in Germany, it was on emergency alert and, as a result, accomplished little operational training. Indeed, a group so close to the Soviet zone was not considered a very good plan. The B-29s of the 301st were on alert to strike immediately if necessary and bomb bases in the Russian-occupied part of Germany.

But just as well, Fürstenfeldbruck—or all the bases of the Americans in their occupation zone—also lay within striking distance of Russian air power. Because of that vulnerability, the group was recalled to the U.S. in early August and replaced by the 2nd Bombardment Group. And the 2nd Group was assigned to the United Kingdom rather than Germany. On August 10, the first B-29s of this group landed on RAF Lakenheath. One squadron was on permanent standby to leave immediately for Fürstenfeldbruck if the situation warranted it. Like the former RAF Bomber Command bases Marham, Waddington, and Scampton, RAF Lakenheath was prepared for the arrival of the heavy B-29 bombers.

This occurred due to a 1942 agreement

between the two countries that allowed the USAAF Eighth Air Force to be stationed in England. By the end of 1946, the last USAAF unit departed from the United Kingdom to the United States; however, the so-called Visiting Forces Act of 1942 remained extant.[95] That Act allowed the American use of 159 airfields in the United Kingdom during the war. Spaatz and Tedder met a couple of times in 1946. What the men concocted then and what bilateral agreements were officially recorded is only partially clear and still shrouded in mist. In the summer of 1946, Spaatz and Tedder must have agreed without public discussion or political debate of the momentous issues.[96]

British bases dire necessity

The fact is that since 1946, provisions were made at airfields in England, and infrastructure was modified to permit the return of heavy American bomber groups of B-29s should the international situation give rise to it. That trigger came in 1948 when Soviet aggression caused a stir in the Allied camp; the blockade of Berlin quickly followed the coup in Czechoslovakia. Both issues aroused fears of spreading communism and made the cracks in the once-intimate Allied alliance abundantly clear. In any case, Spaatz and Tedder's fears were realized in June 1948, giving new impetus to the Anglo-American alliance that laid the groundwork for military cooperation during the Cold War many times of great significance. In 1948, British bases were a dire necessity and formed the basis of U.S. war plans, in which the United Kingdom had a significant role. Indeed, the 1947 Broiler War Plan assumed the destruction of Soviet strategic industrial targets with atomic bombs dropped by B-29s from bases in Egypt, Pakistan, and Britain and B-36s from the US. On May 19, 1948, the Joint Chiefs of Staff (JCS) adopted a modification to Broiler. It became known as Halfmoon, which was the military contingency plan for a hypothetical conflict with the Soviet Union in Europe. The modification involved changes to the size, composition,

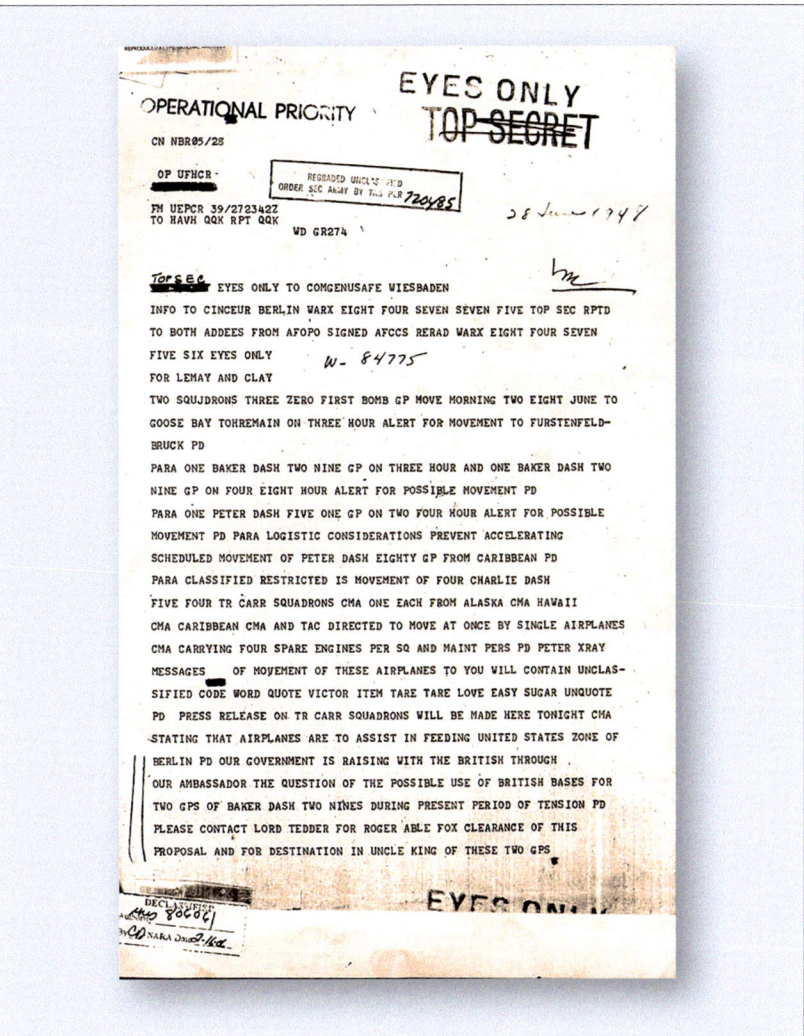

and deployment of U.S. and Allied forces in Europe in the event of a Soviet invasion. It also involved the deployment of U.S. nuclear weapons to Europe, which was a significant escalation in the U.S. military's approach to countering Soviet aggression.

Strategic nuclear offensive

While the Halfmoon modification was a U.S. military decision, it was likely developed in consultation with key U.S. Allies, including the United Kingdom, since, like the original Pincher war plan, it outlined the initial actions from British bases if attacked by the USSR. It concentrated on the first phase, which was a strategic air offensive using atomic weapons against the vital elements of the Soviet war industry. Under

The message from HQ USAF to Lt. Gen. Curtis E. LeMay and Gen. Lucius D. Clay dated June 28, 1948. It concerned the movement of two squadrons of B-29s from the 301st BG to Fürstenfeldbruck Air Base, Germany. The question of basing two groups of B-29s at airfields in the United Kingdom would be raised with the British government. As for transports, the message confirmed that four squadrons of C-54s from Alaska, Hawaii, the Caribbean, and Tactical Air Command had been ordered to Germany. In addition, a fighter group of North American P-51s was placed on alert. However, the message informed the commanders that logistical concerns prevented advancing the deployment of the Lockheed P-80s jet fighter group to Europe. Photo: NARA.

Aviation History Research & Publishing 71

Chapter Six - U.S. Deterrence

In addition to the B-29 bomber response to the Berlin Crisis, SAC deployed RB-29 photoreconnaissance aircraft to Great Britain. Reconnaissance aircraft would play an essential role in the event of hostilities. On August 30, 1948, five RB-29s of the 16th Reconnaissance Squadron (Special) from the 91st Strategic Reconnaissance Group departed McGuire Air Force Base and arrived in England on August 31. They were later joined by another RB-29, bringing the total number of RB-29s in the UK to six. The reconnaissance aircraft were based at RAF Lakenheath, RAF Marham, RAF Scampton, and RAF Waddington.

the expected pressure of mighty Soviet land forces, the Allies would evacuate the European mainland and defend vital bases and lines of communication. In this phase, the UK would have to be held as a staging and operation base for five B-29 groups deployed to delay a Soviet advance in western Europe. In the second phase, the Allies would build up bases in the Middle East and elsewhere in preparation for an ultimate counteroffensive similar in size to the invasion of Normandy in June 1944. The objective of the war would be to cripple or destroy the Soviet Union's war industry. For the strategic air offensive against the Soviet Union, SAC would deploy units to England, Egypt, and Okinawa. If England came under attack and proved untenable, the Allies would shift their bases to Iceland and intensify the use of B-36 intercontinental bombers from bases in Alaska and Greenland. At the outset of a war, SAC's atomic B-29s would start shuttling stockpiled bombs from the Atomic Energy Commission's storage sites in the U.S. to England and the other bases. For that purpose, SAC could, in 1949, source from 170 stockpiled nuclear warheads.[97] At the storage sites, the assembly teams would prepare the atomic bombs. After the bombs were dropped on the targets in the Soviet Union, the bombers would stage back to the United States to collect more nuclear components for assembly at the bases abroad. At least, that was the plan, and the British government agreed to host a B-29 strike force on its soil.

Three B-29 groups based in England

Initially, two groups were approved, but by mid-August, three B-29 Bombardment Groups were stationed in England as part of what SAC called Project Looker. Besides the 2nd at RAF Lakenheath, these groups were the 28th and 307th stationed at RAF Scampton and RAF Marham, respectively, on ninety-day rotations. With this, the Yanks officially returned to England after a two-year absence, and the Anglo-American Alliance was militarily resealed.

Although several former RAF WWII airfields were suitable for nuclear use by the Americans, one would expect SAC to immediately send the 509th Bombardment Group with its atomic bombers to England upon approval by the British Parliament. But that didn't happen. The B-29 had a reputation as an atomic bomber, and at first sight, you could not immediately tell which version could drop a Mark III Fat Man and which was not. The presence of B-29s in England was more of a symbolic value to impress the Russians. The news release accompanying their arrival claimed the ninety or so B-29s were A-bomb capable. Would the Russians have bought into it at the time? Unlikely. The American propaganda machine was blowing up the news that it was non-nuclear bombers who were sent to England. On July 17, the Daily Express drew its readers' attention to the fact that the sixty Superforts were "the type of planes that dropped the atomic bomb on Japan." It was the day the 28th Bombardment Group touched down at RAF Marham, where its commander, Colonel John B. Henri, on arrival, told the press: "We are operational but not primed and cocked," and he added: "We have had nothing to do with atomic bombs."[98]

No A-bombs in Britain, right...?

So no atomic bombers. Or did they? After all, the infrastructure at East Anglia airfields had been modified for use by Very Heavy Bombers (VHBs), including the conventional B-29 and the Silverplate B-29s. Runways were extended, and taxiways and aprons were strengthened to handle the weight of the heavy bombers. There were storage facilities for the nuclear weapons and associated equipment, air-raid shelters, and decontamination facilities to protect personnel from the potential effects of nuclear weapons. It was all in place. So why not include some Silverplate examples among the regular B-29s? If the markings were adjusted, no one would notice. It

also fit with political commentator Drew Pearson's observation two years earlier in The Washington Post that the U.S. stockpiled A-bombs in Northern England, which President Truman strongly denied in his weekly press conference on Friday, October 11, 1946. Pearson was an influential journalist with a nationally circulated column in the 1940s, "Washington Merry-Go-Round," in which he exposed political scandals and intrigue. Less than a month before his expose, he published a politically highly sensitive piece on US Secretary of Commerce Henry A. Wallace. Publicly and in a letter to Truman, the former vice president under Franklin Roosevelt had strongly criticized the U.S. foreign policy. He accused Truman of promoting a "cold war"

On July 17, 1948, the first Boeing B-29 Superfortress landed In Britain for "Temporary Duty" (TDY). Above, a B-29 from the 28th Bombardment Group from Rapid City Air Force Base, South Dakota, touches down at RAF Scampton while a British officer is watching the event. Photo: Alamy.

Below is Boeing B-29A 44-61556 from the 2nd Bombardment Group at Davis Monthan Air Force Base, Arizona. The photo is taken at RAF Lakenheath, Suffolk, England, in August 1948. Together with the 28th BG (to RAF Scampton) and the 307th BG (to RAF Marham), the 2nd BG was relocated from the U.S. to England as part of the U.S. response to the Soviet blockade of Berlin. Photo: U.S. Air Force.

Chapter Six - U.S. Deterrence

mentality which he viewed as a dangerous development that could lead to nuclear war. It met him with fierce criticism from Pearson that had far-reaching consequences: Wallace was expelled from the Democratic Party and had to resign.

Genie out of the bottle

Apparently, with Pearson's revelation of American nukes in England, the genie was out of the bottle again. After a weekend of deliberations, the White House came out with another denial on October 14. Then, Eben Ayers, assistant White House press secretary, was allowed to assure the atomic-worried world on behalf of the President that the U.S. had sent no atomic bombs to England or any other place abroad. "The only atomic bombs that ever got out of the United States were those used in the Bikini test and those dropped on Japan," he said. Ayers commented on a radio broadcast by Drew Pearson the night before, stating again that there were atomic bombs outside the country. "That is untrue," Ayers said, adding that he meant "no bombs, with or without detonators." Several weeks later, the story so vigorously denied by the White House returned to the Washington Post. For, Pearson wrote, as so often happens with diplomatic denials, telltale hints of the truth later leak out. Pearson quoted Senator Tom Connally saying in a public speech, "Canada and Great Britain now possessed the atomic bomb." According to Pearson, it was then possible to report additional details regarding the mysterious shipment of essential atomic bomb parts to Northern England. What was sent by air to England, said Pearson, were the fissile materials—in other words, the explosive parts of the bomb which, when set off, cause so much damage.

According to Pearson, the bomb mechanisms—the detonator devices that set the bombs off—were not shipped to England.[99] Without those mechanisms, the bombs were practically useless. And in case the detonators were indeed supplied, they would need the facilities for the assembly and arming of the nuclear Mark III Fat Man bomb. Would these facilities have been available at RAF bomber bases in Northern England? Or was the lack of it all the more reason in 1947 for developing the Boeing C-97 Chickenpox mobile assembly laboratories? Neither the stockpile in Northern England nor any visiting Chickenpox C-97s have been

A formation of SAC B-29s in 1948 flying over the British countryside. The Superfortresses are of the 28th Bombardment Group from Rapid City Air Force Base, South Dakota, wearing the "Circle R" insignia, similar to the insignia the 6th Bombardment Group during the war and worn by the B-29 Enola Gay that dropped the A-bomb on Hiroshima three years earlier. As part of the SAC Operation Looker these B-29s were on temporary duty deployment to RAF Scampton during the Berlin blockade. Photo: U.S. Air Force/Brian S. Gunderson.

confirmed. The Washington Post stories remain a mystery. But what must Andrei Gromyko, a Soviet diplomat who served as the Soviet Union's representative to the United Nations and later as the Soviet Foreign Minister, have thought of the Washington Post revelations? As recently as October 1946, Bernard Baruch, the U.S. Atomic Energy Commission chairman, had told him that there were no atomic bombs in Canada and England.[100] A year and a half later, during the B-29 deployments to England and Germany, the Russians would have been on the safe side. In that sense, the stationing of "atomic-capable" B-29s worked, even though we know it was probably an American bluff. It all added to the confusion: vigorously denying a press report of A-bomb stockpiling in Northern England; keeping silent when a Senator confirmed the fact; talking about the stationing of atomic-capable B-29s at A-bomb-prepared bases in England; stating on arrival: "We have nothing to do with atomic bombs." These days we call it framing, spinning, and fake news.

What was going on?

One explanation for the turmoil following the Washington Post revelation is that Pearson was wrong and that absolutely no A-bombs were delivered to Britain in 1946. He was merely providing his readers with an insight into the international nuclear chess game, in which vague agreements, intrigue, ignorance, and deception were the main strands. So, what was going on? No doubt it had to do with the Atomic Energy Act of 1946, which determined how the United States would control and manage the nuclear technology it had developed with its World War II Allies, the United Kingdom and Canada. This Act provided that nuclear weapons development and nuclear energy management would be under civilian rather than military control to which the United States Atomic Energy Commission was created. Under the terms of the Act, the U.S. would not share secret information about nuclear weapons with other countries, not even with former Allies such as the United Kingdom.

This move led the British government to resume an independent British program to develop an atomic weapon. The two countries' nuclear paths parted, and before it came to that, the U.S. and Britain agreed in July 1946 to divide the existing uranium reserves in the U.S. roughly equally between them: 1,350 tons each.[101] The British share went to Northern England where there were three nuclear plants. Probably some of the fissile material went to Windscale, located on the Cumbrian coast, which was mainly involved in the production of plutonium for British nuclear weapons.

So, no nukes in England. The assumption is that the Russians knew this all along. Apart from the many American denials—but that might as well have been a bluff—there were, of course, many Russian spies hard at work in England. We remember Klaus Fuchs, the brilliant German/British atomic scientist who, from the highly secret Manhattan program, handed the Russians a complete blueprint of the American bomb. And in 1948, Kim Philby, Guy Burgess, Donald Maclean, Anthony Blunt, and John Cairncross—also known as the Cambridge Five—were working in British intelligence. Philby was head of the Russian intelligence section of the Secret Service MI6 at the time, Maclean was a senior Foreign Office official, and Burgess worked at MI6 as a liaison officer with US intelligence. They shared that they had been spying for the Soviet Union for years. If there had been any nuclear build-up in Britain, Moscow would undoubtedly have been aware of it. And so, the army leadership in Moscow must have viewed the B-29 build-up in England with a very different perspective.

Permanent U.S. presence in Britain

On July 16, 1948, the day before the arrival of the first B-29 squadrons in England, the Third Air Division was established, provisionally, at RAF Marham. Six weeks later, the provisional title was dropped, and on September 8, the headquarters took quarters at Bushy Park, General

NO ATOMIC BOMBS OUTSIDE THE U. S. SAYS PRESIDENT

Announcement Was Made at the White House By Secretary.

ANSWERS DREW PEARSON

Only Atomic Bombs Ever Outside the U. S. Used In the Bikini Test.

WASHINGTON, Oct. 14. (A)—President Truman declared today there are no atomic bombs outside of the United States.

Eben Ayers, assistant White House secretary, asserting he was speaking "on the authority of the President," told a news conference:

"The only atomic bombs ever outside of the United States were those used in the Bikini test and those dropped on Japan."

Ayers made his comment in reply to what he said was an inquiry about a radio broadcast last night by Drew Pearson.

He said the broadcast reported that there are atomic bombs outside this country, and added: "That is untrue."

President Truman told his last news conference that no atomic bombs had been sent to Great Britain.

Ayers said today no bombs are now outside this country, adding that he meant, "no bombs, with or without detonators." "This is on authority of the President."

The White House denial of the Drew Pearson A-bomb story was widely published in the media. In his popular "Merry-go-round" daily column in the Washington Post, Pearson reported that the U.S. had sent atomic bombs to the UK. A story that proved to be untrue.

Chapter Six - U.S. Deterrence

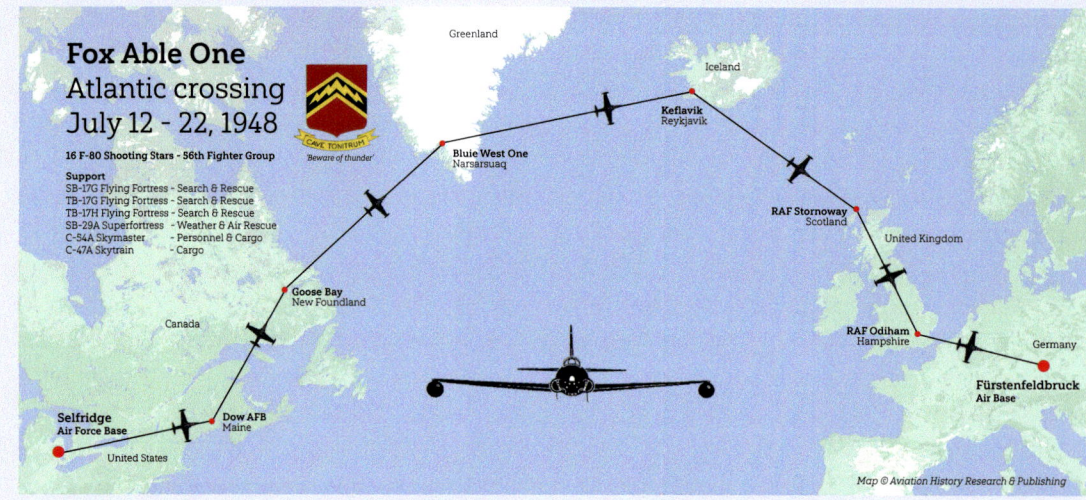

56th Fighter Group crewmembers on the ramp at Goose Bay Air Base. In the center, looking over his shoulder is Lt. Colonel David Carl Schilling - a World War II ace with 22.5 victories. He led the historical ferry flight, which was his idea. He had the personal approval of General Spaatz to demonstrate the feasibility of crossing the Atlantic with fighter jets. The sixteen F-80s that took part in this Fox Able One ferry flight flew from Selfridge AFB, near Detroit, Michigan, to Dow AFB in Maine. From there, they flew to Newfoundland, Greenland, Iceland, Scotland, and finally to RAF Odiham, England, for a goodwill stop. They made it to Germany from RAF Odiham, where they ended up at Fürstenfeldbruck Air Base near Munich. The U.S. Air Force shared the Fox Able One plan with its British Royal Air Force allie. At the same time as the Fox Able One F-80s left Selfridge, a similar flight of six Vickers Vampire Mk.3 jets of RAF No. 54 Squadron left RAF Odiham to the United States, making the same trip in reverse. The two groups crossed paths in Iceland and held a brief ceremony on the tarmac to mark the occasion. The North Atlantic ferry-route became routine in the 1950s when fighter deployments became a regular event. Photo: U.S. Air Force.

When the U.S. Strategic Air Command (SAC) was formed in 1946, its initial mission was to be prepared to conduct long-range offensive operations in any part of the world and to conduct maximum-range reconnaissance over land or sea. When this global responsibility for strategic air operations was given, North American P-51 and Republic F-47 fighter planes provided the strategic bombers with the necessary escort for defense. But soon, the 56th Fighter Group – the command's only fighter wing – was re-equipped with modern Lockheed F-80 jet fighters.

A way had to be found to quickly get these fighters from the U.S. to Europe and the Far East. The answer was, of course, in-flight refueling, but that was still far from perfection. In 1948, SAC started to pioneer the nonstop ocean hops of 900 miles each (1,448 kilometers), which became an accepted routine in the 1950s. The first of the pioneer flights was Fox Able One (Fox for fighter, Able for Atlantic). It was flown in July of 1948 by a 56th Fighter Group F-80 flight from Selfridge AFB in Michigan to Fürstenfeldbruck in Germany.

The flight was not a nonstop strip, and it had its problems. Between Dow AFB, Maine, and RAF Stornoway, Scotland, there were no facilities for jet fighters whatsoever. That omission meant that the refueling filters and other parts and equipment had to be carried along, and due to the exigencies of the Berlin Airlift, there were only two C-54s and one C-47 for transport available.

Execution of Fox Able One took twelve days, including a six-day delay at Goose Bay and overnight stops on Bluie West One (now Narsarsuaq), Keflavik, RAF Stornoway, and RAF Odiham. The 56th Fighter Group remained at Fürstenfeldbruck for two weeks for flight training and flew back to Selfridge, making the same stops as they had made on the way over. Fox Able One was the USAF's first mass overwater deployment of fighter aircraft and was followed in 1949 when fifteen F-80 were flown over to Europe. In 1950, the 27th Strategic Fighter Wing flew 170-odd Republic F-84s over the same route without losing an aircraft.

Source: *Congressional Record, Volume 102, Part 5* (Washington: US Goverment Printing Office) p.6440

Spaatz's former Eighth Air Force headquarters. During WWII, the Third Air Division was part of the Eighth Air Force that finally brought the dreaded Luftwaffe to its knees with strategic precision bombing between 1942 and 1945. So, it was a return of combat forces to England, but this time in peacetime. The Third Air Division was responsible for coordinating the strategic bombing capabilities of the U.S. Air Force in Europe and, to that end, was given jurisdiction over the rotational SAC units in England. It was the first time the USAF had ferried so many fighters simultaneously via the Atlantic ferry route. The jets arrived on July 22, 1948, at the southern German air base after a twelve-day pioneering trip. During their two-week stay, however, the 56th Fighter Group saw little action, and their presence remained primarily a propaganda stunt. The F-80s had come to Western Europe to demonstrate the USAF's ability to deploy a squadron of fighters overseas quickly. By August 14, they had all left to make way for USAFE's planned reinforcements. The 36th Fighter Group, equipped with 80 F-80s in three squadrons, was shipped from Panama to Glasgow in two stages. The first thirteen Shooting Stars arrived aboard the U.S. Army freighter SS Barney Kirchbaum on August 4, 1948, in Glasgow, Scotland.

The Navy aircraft carrier CVE-18 USS Sicily entered port three days later with sixty-nine F-80s on board and most of the group's personnel. The aircraft were disembarked by cranes at the Meadowside of the Clyde River and taken by road—pulled by jeeps—to nearby Renfrew Airport. There the jets went for final assembly and were made airworthy by Scottish Aviation. From Renfrew Airport, the jets flew to Fürstenfeldbruck with stopovers at RAF Manston on the Channel and Wiesbaden Air Base. On August 13, the first F-80s arrived at the air base in Southern Germany. USAFE

On July 12, 1948, sixteen Lockheed F-80 Shooting Stars from the 56th Fighter Group left Selfridge AFB in Michigan for deployment to Fürstenfeldbruck Air Base, Germany. Via the North Atlantic ferry-route, they reached RAF Odiham on 21 July 1948, where this picture was taken of F-80A 44-85321 of the 61st Fighter Squadron.
Photo: U.S. Air Force.

USS Sicily moored in the King George-V docks on the River Clyde. U.S. fighter jets were disembarked by tall cranes and towed over the road to nearby Renfrew Airport. The photo was taken by an RB-26 of the 45th Reconnaissance Squadron at Fürstenfeldbruck Air Base, Germany.
Photo: U.S. Air Force.

Chapter Six - U.S. Deterrence

Lockheed F-80B 45-8600 "40" of the 36th Fighter Group/23rd Fighter Squadron at Fürstenfeldbruck Air Base. On July 2, 1948 the 36th Fighter Wing consisting of a Group with three F-80 squadrons was activated at Howard Air Force Base, Panama Canal Zone. A month later, as a result of the Cold War tensions in Europe, the 36th Fighter Wing was reassigned to United States Air Forces Europe (USAFE) and stationed at Fürstenfeldbruck, Germany. Photo: U.S. Air Force.

put the three squadrons (the 22nd, 23rd, and 53rd Fighter Squadrons) rapidly into readiness at Fürstenfeldbruck. To this end, a training program began immediately to become familiar with the environment and flying conditions in the relatively small European airspace. Germany's airspace then still had the handicap of having to be shared with the other occupying forces. This posed no problem with the French and British, but the Soviet Union was a different story. In those parts of Germany and Austria that they occupied, the Soviet Union only tolerated air traffic in corridors, and anyone outside these corridors could count on a brutal welcome. The American pilots had to get used to this, similar to the European weather conditions, which were quite different from what they were used to on the American continent. So, the new 36th Fighter Group and its jet fighters did not participate in the largest British postwar air exercise. And certainly, neither did the 86th Fighter Group at Neubiberg. The F-47 piston-engined Thunderbolt was no match for the British jets defending their country against the intruding bombers. That meant they were neither a match for the Russian jets whose stationing in the Iron Curtain countries would not be long coming.

Testing the defenses

During August, the B-29 force in the UK had grown to three groups, each with three squadrons of ten operational aircraft; a total of ninety conventional aircraft were prepared and made combat-ready. The USAF built up substantial ammunition stockpiles—Washington ordered as many as 52,000 tons of high explosives and seven million rounds of .50 caliber machine gun ammunition from weapons factories in England. Ground equipment, supplies, and spare parts were shipped from the U.S. to Liverpool, which was more than an indication that the American bombers were over in England for a longer period.[102] In fact, in 1948, the USAF was built on a permanent presence in Britain, a development the Soviets in Moscow had probably not counted on when they turned away from the once-friendly and united Allied alliance with actions in Czechoslovakia and Germany.

General LeMay wanted the B-29s to fly over Britain and continental Europe as frequently as possible. He tried to send a clear message to the Soviets about the strength and readiness of the American military. On weekends during summertime and early fall, the B-29s were scheduled to perform formation flying at low altitudes over major cities and beach resorts in England, Scotland, Wales, and Northern Ireland. In addition, sorties were also scheduled to fly over densely populated areas in continental Europe. Furthermore, practice bombing and gunnery training flights were scheduled for the bombing ranges in the Wash area off the coast of England. And the USAF B-29s in Britain took part in the major British defense exercise held between September 3-7 to test the effectiveness of the UK's air defenses. During the exercise—the biggest since the war—B-29s flew simulated bombing runs under war conditions against targets in the UK while RAF fighters and anti-aircraft defenses attempted to intercept them. The general idea of the exercise imagined an enemy continental power, called Southland, with a western coastline joining Basle, in Switzerland, to the German island of Juist, and thence northwards to a point about halfway up the Norwegian coast. Southland issued an ultimatum to Northland (an area which included the Midlands, East Anglia, and Southeast England) which expired at noon on September 3. The ultimatum was rejected and a declaration of war followed.

The B-29 operated in daylight attacks along RAF Avro Lancaster and Avro Lincoln bombers that also operated at night. The U.S. Third Air Division and RAF Bomber Command formed the air force of Southland that carried

Lockheed F-80B 45-8651 '10' at its dispersal site at Fürstenfeldbruck Air Base in 1949. Facilities at Fürstenfeldbruck were not yet completely ready at the time this photo was taken. At the F-80 flightline, ground staff were still housed in tents and much of the work had to be done in the open. In the distance to the right in the photo, the characteristic white facades of the houses of the village of Maisach, which is directly adjacent to the airfield, can be seen. Photo: U.S. Air Force.

A formation of F-80s, one from each squadron of the 36th Fighter Group, Fürstenfeldbruck. The colours were: 22nd FS Red; 23rd FS Blue; and 53rd FS Green. In the formation are (top to bottom) the F-80Bs 45-8674 "70," 45-8599 "10," and 45-8600 "40." The diagonal red stripes across the fuselage indicate that these are the squadron leaders' aircraft. Photo: U.S. Air Force.

Chapter Six - U.S. Deterence

out mass mock attacks—involving 400-600 aircraft—on the war industries in Coventry, Nottingham, Leicester, Reading, and Swindon. The bomber formations were intercepted by Gloster Meteor IV en De Havilland Vampire Mk.1 fighter jets from RAF Fighter Command. The jets attacked the incoming formations at high speed and high altitude. The result was the virtual downing of some B-29s, and conversely, some defending jets were killed by the Superfortresses; at least, that is how the gun cameras recorded it. In the media, the RAF spoke highly of the defense by the fighter jets it used against the high-flying attackers. But despite the massive defenses, B-29s managed to proceed with their attack. In waves of fifty and more bombers, the virtual targets were all hit; even the War Office in Whitehall, London, was considered obliterated in one raid.[103] United Press reported that the successful mock raids by B-29s from the mythical aggressive Southland proved that Britain couldn't hope for existence if an atomic war broke out. Theoretically, the heart of England lay in almost unprecedented devastation. London would have been a horrifying mass of wreckage if the planes that hit their targets had been carrying atomic bombs.[104] Operation Dagger demonstrated that even against relatively slow-flying atomic bombers, no effective defense was possible. The prospect of jet-powered bombers that could fly as fast as fighters and cruise at high altitudes must have caused unease in the British military leadership. In the US, four such bombers were already in production or an advanced stage of development. Soviet response to these was usually not a long time in coming—quite the contrary. The Answer made its first flight on July 8, 1948. The Ilyushin Il-28 Beagle prototype could make its successful flight thanks to two Rolls-Royce Nene jet engines that the United Kingdom had sold to the Soviet Union. These were the same engines that the Soviets used for their MiG-15 fighter jets. Soviet scientists reverse-engineered the Rolls-Royce Nene; the Soviet copy received the designation RD-45.

Further improvements led to the VK-1, which would be the powerplant of the production Il-28 of which over 6,600 were built for twenty-five air forces. The Il-28 was the first mass-produced jet bomber in the Soviet Union and the basis of a series of jet-propelled Soviet nuclear bombers in the 50s and 60s.

All the result of the extremely ill-considered British technology export deal in 1946 of no less than fifty-five modern Rolls-Royce turbine engines. The Soviet coup in Czechoslovakia and the Berlin blockade were still in the

The Ilyushin IL-28 Beagle is often regarded as the counterpart of the English Electric Canberra, the British first-generation, jet-powered medium bomber. With a top speed of 560 mph (906 km/h) at 15,000 feet (4,500 meters), the Russian jet bomber was faster than the British DeHavilland Vampire jet fighter and just slightly slower than the Gloster Meteor. Photo: VVS.

future, but in 1946 the Soviet Union was still an ally, albeit unpleasant. This foolish action—it would have surprised even Stalin that the British were selling their advanced and secret technology—had far-reaching implications for the balance of power in the Cold War and boosted the arms race between East and West.

B-29 lost over the Netherlands

Operation Dagger was a test of the defense of the British Isles, but it was simultaneously a test of the operational readiness of the new Third Air Division. Above all, the American pilots had to get used to the weather conditions, which were quite different from what they were used to at home. Fog, rain, and low clouds were the typical weather ingredients in much of Europe. And the infrastructure was often different from home; the taxiways and runways were often narrower and shorter, which led to accidents. And unfamiliarity with the environment also played tricks on the pilots.

On September 3, 1948, the first day of the exercise, things went wrong in the bomber formation of the 20th Bombardment Squadron of the 2nd Bombardment Group. The B-29s had taken off from RAF Lakenheath and flown toward the Netherlands. Along the way, they formed into a combat formation. Over Eindhoven in the south of the Netherlands, the formation changed direction; with a large turn and out of range of British radar, the mock attack commenced. Over Brabant, B-29A with serial number 44-62100 went awry. The Superfortress developed engine problems over the Zeeland Islands, and the pilot, 1st Lt. Harold B. Wilson, saw no other option but to give his 10-man crew the order to bail out. They jumped, and all ended up in the waters of the Westerschelde near Vlissingen. According to reports, the unfortunate B-29 ditched near Ritthem between Vlissingen and Borsele. Apparently, the bomber remained afloat for half an hour before sinking into the water 200 feet (60 meters) deep. The ferry Dordrecht and other vessels sent to the rescue took care of the struggling crrew. All but one of the crew survived the crash. Flying at 10,000 feet, the pilot, if had he better known the geographic situation, would have preferred an emergency landing at the former Luftwaffe bomber base Gilze Rijen near Breda, which the formation had passed less than ten minutes earlier.

The heated situation at the time was apparent from the rumor that the B-29 had not ended up in the waters of the Scheldt, but had taken refuge in the Soviet Union. Reputable media, such as the Associated Press, carried the story that the B-29 had been spotted over Hamburg still flying at 10,000 feet, over 300 miles (500 kilometers) from where the crew left the B-29. There was also a report that the bomber had been seen over Lübeck sometime later. In sensational reports, there was even speculation of desertion while the entire crew was recovering from their adventure in Dutch

---

Crewless B-29 From War Game May Have Flown Over Germany

By the Associated Press

FRANKFURT, Germany, Sept. 4.—The possibility that a crewless American B-29 Super Fortress had taken off on a runway flight in the general direction of Moscow held the attention of Air Force officials today.

One thing was certain. A B-29 was missing after its crew of 11 parachuted with the loss of one life yesterday near Flushing off the Netherlands coast while engaged in a mock air war over Britan.

Then came roundabout reports that eyewitnesses had seen a B-29 flying at 10,000 feet over the Hamburg, Germany, area—200 miles away and about an hour after the men jumped.

Other unofficial reports said the plane was seen over Luebeck, about 35 miles northeast of Hamburg.

Air Force officials were inclined to believe the plane fell into the Schelde Estuary where it was abandoned by its crew after engine trouble. One of its rescued crew members said it fell into the water.

But after an intensive search failed to locate any trace of the plane Air Force officials put out on official statement that they were investigating the Hamburg reports.

"It could have happened that way on the time element and everything else," said one airman.

"The plane probably had been set on the automatic pilot before the crew jumped."

Air Force officials refused to speculate on the possibility the plane might reach Russia on its own. Moscow is about 1,600 miles from the spot where the crew jumped. The Super Fortresses have a range of almost 4,000 miles when fully fueled. The B-29 in the Dutch coast incident had been engaged in maneuvers and consequently had used some of its fuel before the crew jumped.

Walter Doyle-Roquet, 21-year-old Tucson (Ariz.) mechanic, who was picked up unconscious by a Flushing fishing boat died in a Dutch hospital early today. Artificial respiration had been applied for many hours.

The other 10 members of the rescued crew were reported in good shape except for shock, bruises and exposure.

The Associated Press reported German sighting reports of an unmanned B-29 flying over Hamburg. Similar sightings also came from the Lübeck area. The story was picked up nationwide by the U.S. media. The press cutting above is from the South Bend Tribune, South Bend, Indiana, dated September 4, 1948.

Chapter Six - U.S. Deterence

hospitals. Would the unmanned B-29 have continued its flight on autopilot (which is on by default during a bailout) in the opposite direction then? Remarkably, although an entire crew was found in the water, despite a search with the deployment of many Royal Netherlands Air Force aircraft, no trace of the B-29 was found in the busy Scheldt estuary. To this day, the fate of B-29 44-62100 remains a mystery.

Air offensive from forward bases

A remarkable aspect of Operation Dagger was that from the USAF only heavy B-29 bombers participated. The fighters that could protect the bombers from the attacking jets, or at least take on the British fighters, stayed in Germany.

In the meantime, the expansion of the American air force in England continued steadily. It had to, if the Americans were ever to implement their Charioteer war plan. Like the previous war plans, Charioteer also assumed that at the start of hostilities the Air Force would begin a strategic air offensive from American bases with long-range B-36 bombers, while B-29s and B-50s would join the attack from secured forward bases.[105] All airfields of the so-called Spaatz/Tedder agreement from 1946 became B-29 bases. These were the RAF air bases Lakenheath, Sculthorpe, Scampton, Mar-ham and Waddington. They were part of the newly formed Third Air Division at Bushy Park, that moved its headquarters in April 1949 to the Victoria Park Estate in South Ruislip, also near London. Service and support to the B-29 force came from the 59th Air Depot that was established at the huge U.S. depot complex at RAF Burtonwood, the largest air base in Europe at the time. RAF Bovingdon, where in October 1945 the first operational B-29 landed, became the Third Air Division's liaison airfield. The first B-29 rotations concerned conventional bombers, not capable of delivering nuclear weapons. During the Berlin crisis, three full groups were constantly on hand in Europe in 1948, because of the emergency. However, in 1949 there was a gradual reduction of Strategic Air Command strength in Europe as the international tension subsided. Yet there was no time in 1949 when at least one full group was not stationed in Europe. The reduction in forces following the Berlin Crisis was a gradual one.

The three-group rotation program gave way to a two-group program, which was in effect from February until August of 1949. In February of 1949, the 92nd and the 307th Bombardment Groups were rotated to Britain.

Shield against fear of aggression

On April 4, 1949, in Washington, twelve nations signed the documents establishing the North Atlantic Treaty Organization (NATO). From that moment, the NATO member states, Belgium, Canada, Denmark, France, Great Britain, Italy, Luxembourg, the Netherlands, Norway, Portugal, Iceland, and the USA, guaranteed each other's safety against outside aggression and saw an armed attack on the territory of one of the member states as an attack on all of them. The signing ink was still wet, when in May the USAF started to replace conventional B-29s on rotation in Great Britain with nuclear-capable Superfortresses. The 509th Bombardment Group that was fully equipped with modified B-29s capable of carrying the Mark III atomic bombs, made its European debut and this time

Boeing WB-29 of the 55th Weather Reconnaissance Squadron, McClellan Air Force Base, California. On September 4, 1949, a B-29 like this one detected a large radioactive cloud over the North Pacific. This photograph was taken on April 30, 1952. Note the air sampling scoop on the aft upper fuselage. The USAF used the so-called "Bug Catcher" to measure radiation levels after surface nuclear weapon tests. The ground crew is hosing off the No. 4 engine during radioactive decontamination. Since the ground crew wears no protective gear, the photo probably shows a procedure test. Photo: U.S. Air Force.

there was no doubt; the U.S. nuclear deterrence had reached East Anglia. Two squadrons of nuclear-capable B-29s were based at RAF Marham and one at RAF Lakenheath. In August, the nuclear rotation was replaced by the USAF's other nuclear-capable group; the 43rd Bombardment Group. In December 1948, the group switched to the Boeing B-50 medium-range Superfortress, a greatly improved version of the WWII B-29, and operated from RAF Sculthorpe, Marham, and Lakenheath. Though the conversion to B-50 aircraft was under way in 1949, the obsolete B-29s continued to be the mainstay of the medium bombardment force of the Strategic Air Command. The capabilities of the B-29s were enhanced by an on-top modification project to allow 180 B-29s to carry atomic weapons. That was about the number of bombers needed to carry out the war plan scenarios of the U.S. and to rain down atomic bombs on the Soviet Union. This was probably what Harry Truman had in mind when he characterized NATO as the shield against fear of aggression. That fear on both sides—East and West—was at the heart of the Cold War and the arms race. It created a legitimate basis for accelerating the military development in both camps. The heat was on.

Joe-1

In September 1948, the U.S. Ambassador in Moscow, General Walter Bedell Smith, assured Washington that, at that moment, the Russians could not possibly have the industrial potential to produce an atomic bomb. According to Bedell Smith, the Russians perhaps had the technical know-how but needed to be able to turn this abstract knowledge into weapons. He thought it would be at least 1953-54 before the Russians could produce an atomic bomb. Nothing was further from the truth because the specialists in Russia's secret nuclear laboratories were already farther ahead than the Americans believed possible. Quietly, without anyone in the Pentagon knowing, the arms race was on and in earnest.

How surprised the military leaders in Washington must have been on September 4, 1949, That day they received a report that a WB-29 operated by the Air Force's Weather Service undertook a routine flight from Misawa Air Base, Japan, to Eielson Air Force Base in Alaska a day during which a large radioactive cloud was observed.[106] The B-29 was on a mission on behalf of the secretive Air Force Office of Atomic Energy-1 (AFOAT-1) and carried a scoop and special filters designed to pick up the radioactive debris that an atmospheric atomic test would inevitably create. The Weather Service operated as many as fifty-five modified B-29s and started scooping the atmosphere for Russian radioactive traces. The operation began in 1948 as part of the U.S. Atomic Energy Detection System. At that time, none of the flights in the Northern Pacific had picked up a scent, but after this flight returned to Eielson and a huge Geiger counter checked the filters, the technicians detected radioactive traces. The filter paper exposed for three hours at 18,000 feet (5.486 meters) showed eighty-five counts per minute on the screen.[107] All alarm bells went off and triggered a complex chain of events, involving more B-29 flights to collect

*The mushroom cloud from the first Russian atomic test. The detonation was on August 29, 1949, at the Semipalatinsk test site in Kazakhstan. This test took aback the Western powers. According to American intelligence, it was anticipated that the Soviets would not develop an atomic weapon until 1953. However, when a U.S. Air Force WB-29 detected the presence of nuclear fission products from the test, the United States promptly initiated the tracking of atomic fallout debris. The 22 kiloton explosion was estimated to be 50% more powerful than anticipated. Five more tests were conducted until March 1950, and the production of bombs equipped with this warhead commenced in December 1951.
Photo: Unknown.*

more air samples, consultations among U.S. government scientists, including radiological analysis by Tracerlab and Los Alamos Laboratory, and, as the radioactive cloud moved east, secret consultations with the British government. The U.S. intelligence community concluded that Moscow had indeed conducted a nuclear test. On September 23, 1949, President Truman announced, "We have evidence that within recent weeks, an atomic explosion occurred in the USSR." According to Pentagon calculations, the detected cloud was from an atomic explosion on the Asiatic mainland between August 26 and 29. The estimate was pretty good since "Joe 1"—as US intelligence designated the first Russian nuclear weapon—was tested on August 29, 1946 at Semipalatinsk, a nuclear test site near Kurchatov in northeastern Kazakhstan.

What do we do about it?

The Russians had managed to reduce their nuclear lag in an impressively short space. Therefore, it is quite possible that the Russians had experimented with atomic weapons far earlier but had escaped the notice of the Americans. Although the USAF's Technical Application Center had been established and given responsibility for the registration of nuclear explosions in the atmosphere some time before, it was not able to start nuclear measurement until the spring of 1949 when reliable measuring instruments that could register nuclear fallout were available.

So how safe was Western Europe at that moment? Was the atomic umbrella under which the NATO member states felt secure big enough? In April 1948, shortly before the Berlin blockade, Strategic Air Command's total nuclear arsenal contained just a little more than thirty atomic bombs. At the end of 1949, the nuclear stockpile had grown to 235 and the Strategic Air Command had 442 bombers to deliver them,[108] more than enough to execute the Charioteer war plan if war broke out. Since 1945, the U.S. had had a nuclear monopoly and the Pentagon believed their hegemony would last until 1953-54. Washington was naturally surprised by the unexpected event in Kazakhstan. The same day President Truman announced the Russian atomic explosion, a secret meeting was held of the Atomic Energy Committee in Washington. It was far from certain what the Russians had other than man-made means of exploding nuclear fission with fast resultant radio reaction.[109] Based on their own experiences, the Americans believed that it would take many months before the Russians could start up production of real bombs. But they also realized that the Russians had many thousands of men at work and the benefit of many top-notch German scientists whom they virtually kidnapped after the war. Literally in a flash, it was a different world with new problems appearing. The meeting ended with two essential questions to be answered: Where do we go from here? And what do we do about it?[110]

Only a little time was given to the Joint Chiefs of Staff in the Pentagon to figure that out. Russia entered the atomic age and turned the Soviet Union into a superpower. Simultaneously, communism rapidly gained ground in Asia, and the world was slowly moving toward the edge. For the Americans, the looming war in Korea was not the right theater for nuclear deployment. Nevertheless, General Douglas MacArthur, the U.S. commander in Korea, intimated the desire to have nuclear weapons at his disposal. He had already drawn up a list of retaliation targets requiring up to twenty-six atomic bombs.[111] Most targets lay in the Cold War's new party: Red China.

By December 31, 1949, the Strategic Air Command (SAC) possessed a total of 837 aircraft, of which 521 were capable of carrying atomic bombs. The photo depicts a formation of North American F-86A Sabre aircraft from the 51st Fighter Interceptor Wing at Suwon Air Base, southwest of Seoul, during a combat mission over Northwest Korea. The Korean War, which took place from 1950 to 1953 and involved significant participation from the Soviet Union and China, hindered the deployment of additional U.S. troops in Europe, while the prospects for postwar rearmament remained uncertain. A substantial portion of the increased military expenditure during this period, as evidenced by the growth of the U.S. defense budget from $14.2 billion in fiscal year 1951 to nearly $66 billion in fiscal year 1952, was allocated to support the Asian conflict.

Despite this focus, Europe continued to be the primary area of concern. However, the conventional defense of Western Europe faced critical shortages in both manpower and equipment. At the beginning of the new decade, the Pentagon estimated that Soviet forces comprised 266 divisions, including 175 line divisions, thirty-five artillery divisions, and fifty-six satellite divisions. Their air power included 20,100 aircraft, including 1,725 long-range bombers capable of reaching targets in North America. The Soviet Navy boasted 400 submarines and 3,225 aircraft. The Soviet military possessed the logistical capability to simultaneously launch attacks on Western Europe, Scandinavia, Italy, the Balkans, Turkey, and the Near East.

Meanwhile, within the NATO alliance, only ten divisions were deployed in West Germany, while defending the Rhine Line required eighteen divisions. Shortages were evident in the alliance's inventory, including a deficit of 8,000 tanks, 9,200 half-tracks, and approximately 3,200 artillery pieces. Consequently, the NATO alliance had to rely on American nuclear weapons in a global conflict. The solution to this predicament was strengthening the coalition and rearming Germany and Japan. The Mutual Defense Assistance Program (MDAP) was established to support NATO and non-aligned countries in containing the Soviet Union. Subsequently, there was a substantial buildup of American forces in Germany, the United Kingdom, and France. Photo: U.S. Air Force.

Chapter One - The Race is On
1. Parrish, Patricia. *Forty-five years of Vigilance for Freedom.* (HQ USAFE, Ramstein air Base: Office of History, 1987), p. 17.
2. Ibid., p. 5.
3. Gosling, Francis G., *The Manhattan Project: making the atomic bomb* (Washington D.C.: US Dept of Energy, 1999), p. 51.
4. Groves, Leslie R., *Now it can be told; the story of the Manhattan project* (New York: Harper & Row Publishers, 1962), pp. 435-346.
5. Ibid., p. 273.
6. Gosling, p. 54.
7. Bohlen, Charles E., *Witness to History 1929-1969* (New York: W. W. Norton, 1973), pp. 247-248.
8. Zkukov, G., *War Memoirs. Reminiscences and Reflections* (Moscow: Progress Publishers. 1974), p. 449.
9. Moorehead, Alan, *The Traitors* (London: Hamish Hamilton, 1952), pp. 58-68.
10. Ibid., p. 85.
11. Ibid., p. 94.
12. Ibid., p. 102.
13. Degroot, G., *The Bomb. A History of Hell on Earth* (London: Pimlico, 2005), p. 126.
14. Smith, Jeffrey K., *Fire in the Sky – The story of the Atomic bomb* (Bloomington: AuthorHouse, 2010), p. 41.
15. Miller Roger G., *Seeing off the Bear. Anglo-American Air Power Cooperation During the Cold War* (Washington, D.C.: Air Force History and Museum Program, 1995), p. 134-135.
16. Norris, Robert S., Cochran Thomas B., *US - USSR/Russian Strategic Offensive Nuclear Forces 1945 – 1996* (Washington: D.C. Natural Resources Defense Council, 1997), table 9.
17. Ross, Steven T., *American War Plans 1945 – 1950* (New York/London: Garland Publishing, 1996), p. 12.
18. Ibid., p. 9.
19. Ibid., p. 14.
20. Ibid., p. 15.
21. Ibid., p. 13.

Chapter Two - Clash over Trieste
22. Polmar, Norman and Bessette, John F., *Spyplanes* (London: Voyager Press, 2016), p. 29.
23. Morrison, M., *442nd remained in Europe after WWII - Mohawk 442nd Fighter Wing Vol. 58, nr 5.* (Kansas: Public Affairs, Whiteman AFB, 2006), p. 10.
24. Shantz, H., Telegram to US Secretary of State, Belgrade, 1946.
25. Jennings, C., *Flashpoint Trieste* (London: Osprey, 2017), p. 275.
26. Hildebrand, John R., *The AACS Naples Detachment of the Army Air Corps, 1943-1947.* In *Air Power History*, Volume 60, Number 2 (Clinton: Air Force Historical Foundation, 2013), p. 13.
27. Jennings, p. 240.
28. Ibid., p. 270.
29. Waarde, Jan van, *Target: Iron Curtain*, accessed January 2023, https://www.16va.be/TargetIronCurtain-JanvanWaarde2010.pdf, p. 4.
30. *U.S. Department of State Bulletin*, Vol. XV, September 1, 1946, p. 415

Chapter Three - Global Capability
31. Moody, Walton S., *Building A Strategic Air Force* (Washington: Air Force History and Museum program, 1995), p. 62.
32. Meilingen, Philips S., *Bomber - The Formation and Early Years of Strategic Air Command* (Montgomery: Air University Press, 2012), p. 97.
33. Hartzer, Ronald B. et al, *Leading the way: the history of Air Force civil engineers 1907-2012* (Frederick: R. Christopher Goodwin & Associates, 2012), p. 77.
34. Abrahamson, James L and Carew, Paul H., *Vanguard of American Atomic Deterrence: The Sandia Pioneers* (Westport, Connecticut: Praeger, 2002), p. 116.
35. Pearson, D., *Washington Merry-go-Round Column* (Washington Post, October 10, 1946).
36. Ross, p. 17.
37. Clay, Lucius D., *Decision in Germany* (London: William Heinemann Ltd., 1950), p. 178.
38. McLaughling, George W., *9th Bombardment Squadron/7th Bombardment Wing*, accessed January 2023, https://www.cbi-history.com/part_vi_9th_bomb_sq.html.
39. Moody, p. 92.
40. Ibid.
41. *Defence's Nuclear Agency 1947- 1997* (Washington D.C.: Defense Threat Reduction Agency, US Department of Defense, 2002), p. 62.
42. Ibid., p. 63.
43. Moody, p. 93.
44. Meilingen, p. 114.
45. Little, Robert D., *Vol. II, Chapter IX Foundations of an Atomic Air Force and Operation Sandstone 1946–1948* (Montgomery: Air University Historical Liaison Office, 1955), p. 391.
46. Moody, p. 93.
47. *SAC Historical Study No. 61, The Strategic Air Command, A chronological History 1946-1956* (Offutt AFB, Nebraska: Historical Division Office of Information HQ SAC, undated), p. 6.

Chapter Four - The Soviet Conduct
48. Ross, p. 63.
49. Rearden, Steven L., *Council of War. Joint Chiefs of Staff* (Washington, D.C.: NDU Press, 2012), p. 70.
50. Condit, Kenneth W., *The Joint Chiefs of Staff and National Policy Volume II - 1947 -1949* (Washington, D.C.: Office of the Secretary of Defense,1976). p. 153.
51. Millis, W., *The Forrestal Diaries* (London: Cassel & Co, 1952), p.196.
52. Perry, M., *Partners in Command* (New York: The Penguin Press, 2007), p. 381.
53. Wilson, Theodore A., *The Marshall Plan an Atlantic venture of 1947-1951 and how it shaped our world. Headline series 236* (New York: Foreign Policy Association, 1977), p. 25.
54. Kahn, Helmut W., *Der Kalte Krieg – Band 1* (Cologne: Paul-Rugenstein Verlag, 1986), pp. 102-103.
55. Clay, p. 159
56. Williamson, D., *Europe and the Cold War* (London: Hodder Education, 2008), p. 54.
57. Millis, p. 363.
58. Ibid., p. 374.
59. Ibid., pp. 366-367.
60. Miller, Roger G., *To Save a City: The Berlin Airlift, 1948-1949* (Williams-Ford Texas A&M University Military History Series, 2000), p.12
61. *Berlin Mission – Report on the Airlift* (Washington: Headquarters Combined Airlift Taskforce, undated), p. 8.
62. Ibid., p. 14.
63. Tusa, John and Ann, *The Berlin Airlift* (New York: Skyhorse Publishing, 2019), p. 118.

Chapter Five - Operation Vittles
64. Samuel, Wolfgang W.E., *I always wanted to fly* (Jackson: University Press of Mississippi, 2001), p. 19.
65. Rodrigo, Robert, *Berlin Airlift* (London: Cassell & Co., 1960), p. 18.
66. Clay, p. 361.
67. Miller, p. 23.

68. Clay, p. 365.
69. Miller, p. 21.
70. Ibid., p. 20.
71. Condit, p. 68.
72. Tusa, p. 150.
73. Lee, Sir David, *The Royal Air Force in Germany 1945-1978* (London: MoD Air Historical Branch, RAF, 1979), p. 8.
74. *Berlin Airlift, a USAFE Summary 26 June 1948 – 30 September 1949* (HQ United States Air Forces in Europe, undated), p. 72.
75. Ibid., p. 122.
76. Miller, p. 34.
77. Rodrigo, p. 58.
78. Wright, K., Jefferies, P., *Looking down the corridors* (Strout, The History Press, 2015), p. 59.
79. Parish, p. 21.
80. Gordon, D., *Tactical Reconnaissance in the Cold War* (Bransley. Pen & Sword Books Ltd, 2006), p. 10.
81. Wright, p. 39.
82. Musser, James M., *Factsheet 45th Reconnaissance Squadron* (Maxwell AFB, Air Force History and Research Agency, 2019).
83. Wright, p. 57.
84. Ibid.
85. Miller, p. 59.
86. Ibid.
87. Steijger, C., *A History of USAFE* (Shrewsbury: Airlife, 1991), p. 70.
88. Berlin Airlift, p. 111.
89. Tusa, p. 257.
90. Donovan, Frank, *Bridge in the Sky* (New York: David McKay Company, 1968), p. 139.
91. Tunner, William H., *Over the Hump* (New York: Duell, Sloan, and Pearce, 1964), p. 199.
92. Miller, p. 116.

Chapter Six - U.S. Deterrence

93. *SAC Historical Study No. 61*, p. 175.
94. Ibid., p. 120.
95. *RAF Airpower Review, Vol.7, No.4* (London: RAF Magazines, 2004), P. 43.
96. Ibid.
97. Norris, Robert S., and Kristensen, Hans M., *Global nuclear weapons inventories, 1945–2010* (Chicago, Illinois: Bulletin of the Atomic Scientists, Jul/au 2010), p. 81.
98. *Herald Express* (Torquay, Devon, England, 17 Jully 1948).
99. Pearson, D., *Washington Merry-go-Round Column* (Washington Post, December 7, 1946).
100. Ibid.
101. Berkemeier, M., Bowen, W.Q., Hobbs, C. and Moran M., *Governing Uranium in the United Kingdom* (Copenhagen: Danish Institute for International Studies, 2014), p. 9.
102. Ibid., p. 126.
103. Command and General Staff College, *Military Review* (Leavenworth, Kansas, 1948), p. 82.
104. Ibid.
105. Ross, p. 80.
106. Condit, Kenneth, *History of the Joint Chiefs of Staff: The Joint Chiefs of Staff and National Policy, Volume II, 1947-1949* (Washington, D.C,: Office of Joint History, Office of the Chairman, Joint Chiefs of Staff, 1996), p. 279.
107. Northrup, Doyle L., Rock, Donald H., *The Detection of Joe 1* (CIA Studies of Intelligence, Volume 10, Issue 4, 1966), p. 23.
108. Norris and Cochran, table 9.
109. Arthur H. Vandenberg, Jr., *The private papers of Senator Vandenberg* (Boston: Hougton Miffling Company, 1952), p. 512.
110. Ibid.
111. DeGroot, p.186

On the Edge - Index

A

ACTS (Air Corps Tactical School) 29
AFSWP (Air Force Special Weapons Project) 37
AFOAT-1 (Air Force Office of Atomic Energy-1) 83
Air Lift Task Force 58, 65
Allied Control Council 48
ATC (Air Transport Command) 21, 22, 56, 61

Air bases

Amendola, Italy 18
Andersen, Guam 69
Andrews, Maryland 41
Barbers Point, Hawaii 36
Brookley, Alabama 65
Bucholz, Marshall Islands 69
Capodichino, Italy 21, 23
Castle Field, California 69
Daugherty Field, California 27
Davis-Monthan, Arizona 23, 37, 38, 70
Dhahran, Saudi Arabia 35, 69
Dow, Maine 76
Eglin, Florida 16
Forth Worth, Texas 28, 36
Fürstenfeldbruck, Germany 18, 24, 33, 34, 35, 43, 44, 60, 61, 62, 64, 68, 69, 70, 71, 72, 76, 77, 78, 79
Fürth, Germany 25, 60
Giebelstadt, Germany 16, 18, 26, 29, 35, 44, 68, 70
Gilze Rijen, Netherlands 81
Goose Bay, Canada 69, 70, 76
Harmon Field, Guam/Mariana Islands 36
Hickham, Hawaii 69
Hsinchu, Taiwan 24
Kadena, Okinawa 18, 19, 38
Kastrup, Denmark 14
Keflavik, Iceland 69, 76
Kirtland Field, New Mexico 38
Kitzingen, Germany 26
Ladd Field, Alaska 29
LaGuardia, New York 27
Lajes, Azores 23, 35, 65, 69
Le Bourget, France 35
Lesce, Slovenia 22
Lesina, Italy 26
Louisville, Kentucky 24
MacDill, Florida 69, 70
March, California 30, 39
McGuire, New Jersey 29, 34, 72
Morrison Field, Florida 23
Neubiberg, Germany 44, 78
North Field, Tinian/Mariana Islands 11, 30, 36
Nordholz, Germany 26
North West Field, Guam/Mariana Islands 11, 30, 36
Orly, France 14, 35
RAF Bassingbourn. England 31
RAF Bovingdon, England 14, 82
RAF Broadwell, England 49
RAF Bückeburg, Germany 52
RAF Burtonwood, England 26, 64, 82
RAF Celle, Germany 52, 56, 58, 59, 64
RAF Detmold, Germany 52
RAF Duxford, England 13
RAF Fassberg, Germany 52, 56, 58, 59, 63, 64
RAF Gatow, Germany 48, 49, 52, 54, 58, 60, 62, 63, 65
RAF Glatton, England 31
RAF Grafton Underwood, England 45
RAF Greenham Common, England 69
RAF Gütersloh, Germany 52
RAF Horsham, England 31
RAF Kharagpur, India 31
RAF Knettishall, England 31
RAF Lakenheath, England 18, 19, 34, 37, 38, 70, 72, 73, 81, 82, 83
RAF Marham, England 16, 17, 18, 19, 29, 35, 38, 70, 72, 73, 75, 82, 83
RAF Mildenhall, England 18, 29
RAF Northolt 60
RAF Odiham, England 76, 77
RAF Scampton, England 17, 18, 19, 38, 70, 72, 73, 74, 82
RAF St. Mawgan, England 31
RAF Stornoway, Scotland 76
RAF Ueterese, Germany 49
RAF Wunstorf, Germany 52
Renfrew Airport, Scotland 77
Rhein-Main, Germany 18, 23, 29, 32, 47, 48, 51, 52, 56, 57, 58, 59, 61, 63, 64
Riem/Munich, Germany 21
Roswell Field, New Mexico 30
Sandia Base, New Mexico 37, 86
Schiphol, Netherlands 14
Schönefeld, Germany (east) 48, 54
Selfridge, Michigan 76, 77
Shemya Island, Alaska 69
Smoky Hill, Kansas 29, 35, 37, 43, 69, 70
Staaken, Germany (east) 48, 54
Tegel, Germany 54, 58, 63, 64, 65
Tempelhof, Germany 2, 46, 48, 49, 51, 52, 54, 56, 57, 58, 59, 60, 61, 62, 63, 65, 66
Tulln/Langenlebarn, Austria 21
Udine, Italy 21, 22, 25
Westover, Massachusetts 65, 69
Wiesbaden, Germany 24, 48, 49, 52, 56, 57, 58, 59, 61, 62, 63, 64, 65, 77
Wissawa, Japan 18
Yokota, Japan 18, 19, 29, 36, 68, 69

Aircraft

AVRO Lancaster 79
AVRO Lincoln 79
AVRO York 52
Bell P-39 Airacobra 21
Boeing B-29 Superfortress 11, 14, 15, 16, 17, 18, 19, 23, 25, 26, 29, 30, 31, 32, 33, 34, 35, 36, 37, 38, 39, 40, 41, 43, 44, 45, 48, 51, 66, 68, 69, 70, 72, 73, 74, 75, 78, 79, 81, 82, 83
Boeing C-97 Chickenpox 37, 38, 74
Boeing C-97 Stratofreighter 37, 74
Boeing F-9 Flying Fortress 21, 24
Boeing F-13 Superfortress 21, 29, 33, 34
Boeing RB-17 Flying Fortress 21, 64
Boeing RB-29 Superfortress 29, 33, 34, 43, 60, 68, 72
Consolidated F-7 Liberator 21
Consolidated RB-24 Liberator 21
De Havilland Vampire Mk.1 80
Douglas A-26 Invader 30, 44, 60
Douglas C-47 Skytrain 20, 21, 22, 25, 42, 46, 47, 48, 49, 53, 55, 57, 58, 64, 76
Douglas C-54 Skymaster 11, 34, 36, 48, 49, 53, 56, 58, 59, 60, 61, 63, 64, 65, 67
Douglas C-74 Globemaster I 63
Douglas C-124 Globemaster II 66
Douglas F-3 Invader 21
Douglas R4D Skytrain 57
Douglas R5D Skymaster 64
Douglas RB-26 Invader 21, 64, 77
Fairchild C-82 Packet 63, 64, 65
Gloster Meteor IV 80
Gurevick MiG-9 27
Ilyushin IL-28 Beagle 80
Junkers Ju-52 54, 55, 65
Lockheed C-69 Constellation 53
Lockheed P-2V Neptune 24
Lockheed P-80R Shooting Star 27
Lockheed YP-80 Shooting Star 26
Messerschmitt Me-262 27
Mikoyan-Gurevich MiG-15 Fagot 27, 80
North American P-51 Mustang 44, 60
North American T-6 Harvard/Texan 64
Short Sunderland 52
Tupolev Tu-4 33, 40
Yakolev Yak-3 21, 22, 25, 48, 62

B

Berlin corridors 21, 29, 43, 48, 53, 58, 59, 60, 61, 62, 63, 65, 78, 87
Buzzing (corridors) 48, 62

C

CALTF (Combined Airlift Task Force) 54, 65, 89
Chaff 62
Chickenpox (C-97) 37, 38, 74
CIA 24, 43, 87
Currency reform 49, 50, 51

E

EATS (U.S. European Air Transport Service) 21
ELINT (Electronic Intelligence) 21, 24, 25, 29, 61
EUCOM (U.S. Army European Command) 51

F

Fat Man 11, 13, 17, 18, 34, 37, 73, 74
Ferret 20, 25, 29, 61

G

GCA (Ground Control Approach) 59, 60, 63

Individual aircraft

41-36393 YB-29A Superfortress Hobo Queen 14, 31
42-13570 XB-36 Peacemaker 28
42-63577 B-29A Superfortress 16
42-65414 C-74A Globemaster I 65
42-72452 C-54D Skymaster 63
42-92467 C-47A Skytrain 51
42-92841 C-47A Skytrain 48
43-15075 C-47A Skytrain 20
43-15672 C-47A Skytrain 57
43-17223 C-54D Skymaster 49
43-27470 XC-97 Chickenpox Stratofreighter 37
44-9030 C-54E Skymaster 63
44-27354 B-29A Superfortress 'Dave's Dream' 17
44-33457 F-47D Thunderbolt 79
44-35914 RB-26C Invader Hot Lips 60
44-61556 B-29A Superfortress 73
44-61679 B-29A Superfortress 14, 29
44-61822 F-13 Superfortress 33
44-61938 B-29A Superfortress 35
44-62100 B-29A Superfortress 81, 82
44-85123 P-80R Shooting Star 27
44-85321 F-80A Shooting Star 77
44-85365 F-80C Shooting Star 39
44-85531 RB-17 Flying Fortress 24
44-85541 F-9C Flying Fortress 24
44-86292 B-29A Superfortress Enola Gay 11, 30, 74
44-89817 F-47D Thunderbolt 44
44-89869 F-47D Thunderbolt 44
44-89985 F-47N Thunderbolt 79
44-92010 B-26A Peacemaker 41
45-527 C-54G Skymaster 67
45-549 C-54G Skymaster 57

45-649 C-54G Skymaster 63
45-8600 F-80B Shootin Star 78, 79
45-8628 F-80B Shooting Star 4
45-8651 F-80B Shooting Star 79
45-8674 Shooting Star 79
45-8699 Shooting Star 79
45-21747 B-29A Superfortress 16
45-21750 B-29A Superfortress 16
45-21751 B-29A Superfortress 16
45-21812 RB-29A Superfortress 'Sitting Duck' 29
45-57791 C-82A Packet 63
45-59587 YC-97 Chickenpox Stratofreighter 37
45-59589 YC-97 Chickenpox Stratofreighter 37
45-59592 YC-97 Chickenpox Stratofreighter 37, 86
46-065 XB-47 Stratojet 69
47-011 B-45A Tornado 68
48-096 B-50D Superfortress 31
50-649 F-86E Sabre 85
50-793 F-86E Sabre 85
51-2793 F-86E Sabre 85
52-0412 EB-47E Stratojet 69
53-7885 VC-121E Constellation 'Columbine III' 53

J
JCS (Joint Chiefs of Staff) 19, 71
JSPG (Joint Strategic Planning Group) 40, 41
JSSC (Joint Strategic Survey Committee) 19
JWPC (Joint War Plans Committee) 18, 19, 22, 34, 38, 41

K
Kremlin 25, 27, 41, 45, 55, 56

L
Little Boy 11, 13, 30, 32, 37

M
MATS (Military Air Transport Service) 53, 56, 57, 63
MDAP (Mutual Defense Assistance Program) 64, 85
Morgan Line 23, 25

N
NATO (North Atlantic Treaty Organization) 82, 83, 84

Operations
Operation Vittles 49, 50, 51, 52, 54, 56, 57, 58, 60, 61, 62, 64, 65, 66, 86
Operation Carter Paterson 52
Operation Crossroads 17, 33
Operation Dagger 80, 81, 82
Operation Finback 36
Operation Knicker 52
Operation Little Lift 47, 48, 52
Operation Looker 74
Operation Pacific 35
Operation Plainfare 52, 54, 57, 65
Operation Sandstone 86
Operation Squirrel Cage 53
Operation Sunfast 69, 70

P
Pacusan Dreamboat (B-29) 25
Pentagon 35, 38, 41, 45, 50, 51, 83, 84, 85

People
Attlee, Clement, British prime minister 7, 10, 75
Ayers, Eben, U.S. ass. White House press secretary 74
Baruch, Bernard, Chairman U.S. Atomic Energy Commission 75
Bevin, Ernest British foreign secretary 43, 51, 70
Bieri, Bernhard H., U.S. admiral 23
Blunt, Anthony, British spy 75
Bohlen, Charles E., author 11
Bohlen, Charles E., U.S. interpreter 11, 86, 90
Burgess, Guy, British spy 75
Byrnes, James, U.S. secretary of state 10, 14
Cairncross, John, British spy 75
Chamberlin, Stephen J., U.S. director of intelligence 46
Churchill, Winston, British prime minister 9, 14, 15
Clay, Lucius D., U.S. military governor West Germany 44, 46, 47, 48, 49, 50, 51, 52, 62, 63, 70, 71, 86, 87
Clayton, William L., U.S. secretary of state 25
Councill, William H., U.S. colonel 25
Eaker, Ira C., U.S. general 29
Eisenhower, Dwight D., U.S. general/president 9, 41, 42, 46, 47
Forrestal, James V., U.S. secretary of defense 45, 86
Foster, John, U.S. secretary of state 53
Fuchs, Klaus, German/British physicist 14, 15, 75
Göring, Helmut, Field marshal (Luftwaffe) 55
Gromyko, Andrei, Soviet diplomat 75
Groves, Leslie R., U.S. general 13
Henri, John B. Colonel, USAF 73
Hirohito, Japanese emperor 13
Irvine, Clarence S., U.S. colonel 25
Kelly Johnson, Lockheed developer 26
Keyes, Geoffrey, commander U.S. Forces Austria 53
Kurchatov, Igor W., Soviet nuclear scientist 14, 15, 84
Le May, Curtis E., U.S. general 29, 56, 63
Maclean, Donald, British spy 75
Marshall, George, U.S. secretary of state 23, 35, 43, 45, 49, 69, 86
Masaryk, Jan, Czech foreign minister 45
McNarney, Joseph, U.S. general 9, 32
Mitchell, Billy, U.S. general 28, 29
Molotov, Vyacheslav, Soviet foreign minister 10, 11, 14, 18, 19, 23, 38, 41
Morgan, Sir William Duthie, British general 23, 25
Nichols, Philip, British anbassador Prague 45
Oppenheimer, Robert, U.S. scientist 13, 14
Patton, George, U.S. general 32
Pearson, Drew, journalist/commentator 73, 74, 75, 86, 87
Philby, Phil, British spy 75
Pieck, Wilhelm, German Communist leader 47
Robertson, Sir Brian, British military commander West Germany 50
Roosevelt, Franklin D., U.S. president 9, 10, 23, 29, 47, 73
Schilling, David C., Lt. colonel, USAF 76
Sokolovsky, Vassily D., Soviet military governor Berlin 49
Spaatz, Carl, U.S. general 6, 7, 25, 29, 30, 31, 34, 71, 76, 77, 82
Stalin, Joseph, Communist leader 7, 10, 25
Swancutt, Woodrow P., U.S. major 17
Sweeney, Charles W., U.S. major 11
Tedder, Sir Arthur, British air chief marshal 34
Tibbets, Paul W., U.S. colonel 11
Tito, Josip Broz, Yugoslav Communist leader 23, 25
Truman, Harry S., U.S. president 7, 13, 15, 25, 39, 41, 50, 83
Tunner, Henry, U.S. general 56, 57, 58, 59, 61, 65, 66, 87
Vodopivec, Vladimir, pilot Yugoslav Air Force 21
Wallace, Henry A., US secretary of Commerce 73, 74
Wilson, Harold B., 1st Lt. 81, 86

Places
Alamogordo, New Mexico 9, 13, 15, 33
Baku, Azerbaijan 18, 19, 38
Baltic Sea 29
Bering Strait 29, 69
Berlin, Germany 1, 4, 9, 10, 13, 21, 24, 29, 35, 43, 44, 46, 47, 48, 49, 50, 51, 52, 53, 54, 55, 56, 57, 58, 59, 60, 61, 62, 63, 64, 65, 66, 69, 70, 71, 72, 73, 74, 76, 81, 82, 84, 86, 87
Bikini, Pacific 17, 33, 34, 74
Bled, Yugoslavia 22, 25
Brabant, Netherlands 81
Brenner Pass, Austria 22
Calabria, Italy 22
Chelyabinsk, Russia 18, 19, 38
Copenhagen, Denmark 14, 35, 40, 87
Dordrecht, Netherlands 81
Farge, Germany 16
Foggia, Italy 18, 19, 26, 32
Gorki, Russia 18, 19, 38
Grozny, Chechnya 18, 19, 38
Guam, Mariana Islands 29, 36, 56, 57, 69
Hamburg, Germany 16, 49, 54, 81
Helgoland, Germany 16
Hiroshima, Japan 6, 7, 11, 13, 17, 30, 32, 37, 39, 45, 69, 74
Honshu Island, Japan 11
Irkutsk, Russia 19
Kamchatka peninsula, Russia 29
Kazan, Russia 18, 19
Klagenfurt, Austria 22
Kokura Arsenal, Japan 11, 13
Kranj, Yugoslavia 22, 25
Kuibyshev, Russia 18, 19, 38
Kyushu Island, Japan 13
Laibach/Ljubjana, Yugoslavia 22
Leningrad, Russia 18, 19, 38
Los Alamos, New Mexico 13, 15, 30, 84
Magnitogorsk, Russia 18, 19, 38
Mariana Islands, Pacific 11, 36
Molotov, Russia 10, 11, 14, 18, 19, 23, 38, 41
Moscow, Russia 9, 17, 18, 19, 25, 27, 33, 38, 39, 40, 41, 43, 45, 48, 50, 55, 75, 78, 83, 84, 86
Nagasaki, Japan 7, 13, 17, 29, 32, 37, 39, 45
Neuengamme, Germany 16
Nizhni Tagil, Russia 18, 19, 38
Novosibirsk, Russia 18, 19, 38
Omsk, Russia 18, 19, 38
Pearl Harbor, Hawaii 13, 46
Potsdam, Germany 7, 10, 14, 15, 16, 33, 41, 46, 47, 48
Quebec, Canada 9
Sainte-Mère-Église, France 51
Sait-Mahiel 28
Saint-Nazaire, France 16
San Francisco, California 10
Saratov, Russia 18, 19, 38, 69
Sarov, Russia 41
Scheldt, Netherlands 82
    Westerschelde 81
Semipalatinsk, Kazakhstan 15, 83, 84
Stalinsk, Russia 18, 19, 38
Stettin, Poland 10
Sverdlovsk, Russia 18, 19, 38
Swinemünde, Poland 10
Tashkent, Uzbekistan 18, 19
Tbilisi, Georgia 18, 19, 38
Teheran, Iran 9
Tinian Island, Pacific 6, 7, 11, 30, 37
Trieste, Italy 20, 22, 23, 24, 26, 86
Venezia-Giulia district, Italy 22
Vienna, Austria 15, 21, 24, 25, 46, 53

On the Edge - Index

Places continued
Vlissingen, Netherlands 81
    Borselen 81
    Ritthem 81
Yalta, Krim 9
Yaroslavl, Russia 18, 19
Zeeland islands, Netherlands 81

Projects/Programs

Project Barbara 34
Project Casey Jones 21, 25
Project Extraversion 26
Project Harken 16
Project Looker 72
Project Manhattan 9, 13, 14, 15, 38, 75, 86
    Project W-47 38
Project Ruby 16
Project Wonderful 31, 32

R
Reichstag 14

S
SAC (Strategic Air Command) 17, 25, 29, 30, 31, 32, 33, 35, 36, 37, 38, 39, 41, 44, 69, 70, 72, 73, 74, 76, 77, 82, 83, 84, 85, 86, 87
Silverplate B-29 16, 17, 33, 35, 38, 69, 73
Skunk Works 26
Socialist German Unity (SED) 47

T
Truman Doctrine 41, 42

Units

1st Air Transport Unit, USAF 34, 37
1st Reconnaissance Squadron, USAF 34, 37, 39, 60, 81
7th Bomb Group, USAF 35
10th Air Depot, USAF 64
10th Headquarters and Base Services Squadron, USAF 24, 64
10th Reconnaissance Group, USAF 60
10th Tactical Carrier Squadron, USAF 24, 25, 60, 61, 62, 64
11th Tactical Carrier Squadron, USAF 64
12th Tactical Carrier Squadron, USAF 63, 64
14th Tactical Carrier Squadron, USAF 64
15th Tactical Carrier Squadron, USAF 64
16th Photographic Reconnaissance Squadron, USAF 33, 34, 43
20th Troop Carrier Squadron 49
22nd Fighter Squadron, USAF 64, 72, 78
23rd Fighter Squadron, USAF 36, 64, 78, 79
28th Bombardment Group, USAF 35, 58, 70, 72, 73, 74
30th Mobile Repair Squadron, USAF 26
31st Fighter Group, USAF 26
34th Black Bat Squadron, Republic of China Air Force 24
36th Fighter Group, USAF 61, 64
38th Engineer Battalion, U.S. Army 37
39th Tactical Carrier Squadron, USAF 64
40th Tactical Carrier Squadron, USAF 29, 64
41st Tactical Carrier Squadron, USAF 64
43rd Bombardment Group, USAF 23, 38, 70, 83
45th Reconnaissance Squadron, USAF 44, 60, 61, 64, 77, 87
45th Tactical Reconnaissance Squadron, Night Photographic, USAF 61
53rd Fighter Squadron, USAF 48, 64, 78
53rd Tactical Carrier Squadron, USAF 48, 64, 78
53rd Troop Carrier Squadron, USAF 48
56th Fighter Group, USAF 76, 77
58th Bombardment Wing, USAF 30, 37
60th Tactical Carrier Group, USAF 48, 51, 56, 64
85th Air Depot Wing, USAAF 64
86th Composite Wing, USAF 61
86th Fighter Group, USAF 44, 64, 78, 79
88th Infantry Division, U.S. Army 23
91st Strategic Reconnaissance Group, USAF 33, 34, 72
92nd Bombardment Group, USAF 82
97th Bombardment Group, USAF 16, 29, 35, 37, 39, 44, 70
301st Bombardment Group, USAF 43, 69, 70
301st Troop Carrier Squadron, USAF 46
305th Troop Carrier Squadron 21, 22, 45
307th Bombardment Group, USAF 35, 70, 82
311th Air Division, USAF 33, 68
311th Reconnaissance Wing, USAF 21
324th Radio Countermeasures Squadron, USAF 29
330th Tactical Carrier Squadron, USAF 64
331st Tactical Carrier Squadron, USAF 64
333rd Tactical Carrier Squadron, USAF 64
340th Bombardment Squadron, USAF 29, 35
393rd Composite Squadron, USAF 69
439th Troop Carrier Group, USAF 20
442nd Troop Carrier Group, USAF 21, 86
492nd Bomb Squadron, USAF 35
509th Composite Group, USAF 6, 7, 11, 13, 17, 29
509th Bombardment Group, USAF 30, 37, 38, 39, 69, 73, 82
525th Fighter Squadron, USAF 64
526th Fighter Squadron, USAF 64
527th Fighter Squadron, USAF 44, 64
7165th Composite Group 63
7169th Weather Reconnaissance Squadron, USAF 61, 64
7200th Air Force Depot Wing, USAF 64
7280th Air Base Group, USAF 64
7290th Air Base Group, USAF 64
7300th Air Force Composite Wing, USAF 61
7360th Base Complement Squadron, USAF 64
7405th Support Squadron, USAF 24
7499th Air Force Squadron, USAF 62, 64, 90
7499th Composite Squadron, USAF 62, 69, 90
Jagdgeschwader 4, Luftwaffe 32
Luftnachrichten-Regiment 248, Luftwaffe 25
No. 35 Squadron, RAF 35
No. 77 Squadron, RAF 49
No. 201 Squadron, RAF 52
VR-6, US Navy 64
VR-8, US Navy 64

U
University of Bristol 15
USAFE (U.S. Air Forces in Europe) 11, 20, 22, 24, 25, 26, 30, 32, 42, 43, 44, 47, 48, 60, 61, 62, 69, 77
USFEAF (U.S. Far East Air Force) 36, 69
U.S. Joint Chiefs of Staff 19, 71, 84, 86, 87
U.S. Joint Intelligence Committee 18
U.S. Joint Strategic Survey Committee 19
U.S. Joint War Plans Committee 18, 19, 22

V
Valentin (bunker), Germany 16

Vessels
USS Barney Kirchbaum 77
USS Cone 23
USS Corry 23
USS Fargo 23
USS Franklin D. Roosevelt 23
USS Little Rock 23
USS New 23
USS Power 23
USS Sicily 77
USS Small 23

W
WEU (Western European Union) 66

Warplans
Broiler 38, 41, 71
Bushwacker 38
Charioteer 38, 82, 84
Halfmoon 38, 71
Pincher 19, 24, 30, 38, 71